Study skills for 14–16 year-olds

Studywise 2

John Foster

Collins Educational

An imprint of HarperCollins*Publishers*

Published in 1996 by Collins Educational
An imprint of HarperCollins*Publishers*
77-85 Fulham Palace Road
Hammersmith
London W6 8JB

www.**Collins**Education.com
On-line support for schools and colleges

ISBN 0 00 320189 9

Designed by Stuart Perry

Cover illustration by Mike Moran

Internal illustration by Adrian Barclay (Behive Illustration) pp6,12,28 & 49, Mike Moran pp5,8,12,13,26 & 42, Mike Parsons (Barking Dog Art) pp9,11,16,17,19,25 & 59, Clyde Pearson pp7 & 45, Francis Scappaticci (Maggie Mundy Illustration Agency) pp18,19,31,32 & 58, Harry Venning pp7,10,23,30,34,41 & 53.

Handwriting by Alice Bradbury, Katy Bradbury.

Commissioning Editor Graham Bradbury

Editor Louisa Coulthurst

Printed and Bound by Printing Express Ltd., Hong Kong.

ACKNOWLEDGEMENTS

The following publishers, authors and agents are thanked for permission to reproduce extracts and copyright material:

Addison Wesley Longman for the questions and answers on common myths about exams pp40 & 41 from *GCSE Survival Guide* by Nicky Hayes.

Cassell for information on the format of a technical report p31 from *How to Succeed at GCSE* by John Bowden.

City and Guilds for the information about GNVQs pp62 & 63 from *GNVQs - A Guide for Students*.

English & Media Centre for the information on claptraps p34 from the article *Making Speeches* by Barbara Bleiman from Issue 24 of *The English Magazine*.

HarperCollins*Publishers* Ltd for the extract from *Co-ordinated Science GCSE Book 2* edited by Ken Dobson p19 and the personal qualities checklist p52, the statements by Coretta and Tim p52 and the list of qualities needed in various areas of work p53 from *Working on it: Thinking about jobs* by Jenny Thewlis.

Hobsons Publishing PLC for the qualifications framework chart p59 from *The Parents' and Guardians' Guide to GCSE Options and Beyond* and the table comparing GNVQs and NVQs p64 from *GNVQ: is it for you?* For further information about CRAC/Hobsons' publications, please contact Alice Marshall, Customer Services on 01223 464334.

London Examinations for the exam papers p36.
Midland Examining Group for the exam papers p36.
Northern Examinations and Assessment Board for the exam papers p36.

Oxford University Press for the extract on superstores p20 from *A New Geography of Britain* by Rex Beddis.

Reed Educational and Professional Publishers Ltd for the list of abbreviations p24 and tables A and B p25 from *Study Skills for Reading* by Evelyn Davis and Norman Whitney published by Heinemann Educational Books.

Stanley Thornes (Publishers) Ltd for the extract about Data Collection p15 and the information and graphs about the GCSE Geography enquiry pp16 & 17 from *GEO* magazine and for the extract on immunisation p23 from *Key Science: Biology* by David Applin.

The following are thanked for permission to reproduce photographs:

Asda p20
Roger Bradley and National Council for Vocational Qualifications p62
HarperCollins*Publishers* Ltd p29
Jennie Woodcock, Reflections Photo Library pp4,13,46,60

Every effort has been made to contact owners of copyright material but if any have been inadvertently overlooked the publishers wil be pleased to make the necessary arrangements at the first opportunity.

CONTENTS

Introduction

How this book can be used

Studywise 2 is planned so that it can be used in a variety of ways. It can be used in schools either as a separate course on study skills within a school's tutorial programme or integrated within a school's personal and social education programme. Alternatively, you can use it on your own or work through it with a friend or member of your family. Since each of the units deals with a separate topic, they can be worked through in any particular order, according to your own personal needs.

What this book is about

Studywise 2 is the second of two books designed to help you to develop the skills you need in order to succeed in the subjects you are studying between the ages of 14 and 16. The book is divided into twelve units offering practical advice on how to develop the skills that will enable you to work effectively when doing supported self study and to perform to the best of your ability in your lessons, in your coursework and tests, and in the examinations that you have to take.

The information and the activities in the units are designed to help you:
● to think about how you learn;
● to learn how to take responsibility for your own learning;
● to develop the skills that will enable you to study effectively and pass your examinations;
● to identify your strengths so that you can decide which courses you want to take and which pathway you want to follow at 16+.

Study skills and your examination courses

Between the ages of 14 and 16, you will be studying a range of different subjects. The subjects you are doing will depend to a certain extent on the courses you have chosen, but everyone must do English, Maths and Science. In addition you will have to do a Modern Language, Technology and R.E., and in many schools, you may have a regular Personal and Social Education lesson.

In each of the subjects you are studying, you will be learning particular skills. For example, in Science you will be learning the skills of observation and investigation. In English, you will be learning how to write essays and how to interpret texts.

Study skills differ from subject skills, because they do not apply to one specific subject. They are techniques that you can use to help you to learn in any subject. Study skills include planning and organising your time, developing your reading strategies, learning how to take notes and how to revise for examinations.

It is important to develop your study skills for a number of reasons. First, improving your study skills will help you to improve your examination grades. Second, it will save you time and effort by making your studying more efficient.

What study skills do I need to learn?

1 How to manage your time

The key to successful studying is planning and organisation. When they start examination courses, many students find it hard to cope with the amount of work they have to do. **Unit 1** offers advice on how to plan and organise your study time and how to develop good study habits.

2 How to find and collect information for coursework projects

For your coursework you will need to be able to find information in a library, access information from computers, carry out surveys and questionnaires and conduct interviews. You will also need to be able to analyse and present the data that you collect. **Unit 2** will help you to develop these skills.

3 How to learn from books and other sources of information

Once you have found the information you want, you need to have the skills necessary to be able to learn from it by extracting and recording the relevant facts and ideas. **Units 3** and **4** will help you to do this.

4 How to communicate facts, ideas and opinions

You need to be able to show that you have understood what you have learned by speaking and writing about it. Being able to communicate information and to express your ideas and opinions are two very important study skills. **Unit 6** will help you to develop your oral skills – to give talks and to present arguments in debates. **Unit 5** will help you to develop your essay-writing skills.

5 How to revise

As the examinations approach, it is essential to plan your time and to use an effective revision technique. **Unit 7** explains how to draw up a revision calendar and how to develop an active approach to revision.

6 How to cope with examinations

Many students find preparing for and taking examinations stressful. **Unit 8** offers advice on how to cope with exam pressures and **Unit 9** describes techniques you can develop for tackling examination papers.

7 How to review your progress

Thinking about what you have learned and the skills you have developed is useful because it helps you to realise what you have achieved and enables you to think about what you still need to learn. **Unit 10** provides you with an opportunity to assess your study skills and your progress in each of your subjects, and shows you how to prepare your personal statement for your Record of Achievement.

8 How to make decisions about careers and your future education

At 16, you will have to decide whether to continue your education or to receive training for a job. **Unit 11** will help you to think about careers and the qualifications you need for different jobs. **Unit 12** explains the options that are available at 16+ and what the consequences of particular choices can be.

1 Managing your time

TIME-MANAGEMENT

IN PAIRS

Discuss the subjects you are studying. Tell each other in which subjects you find it easy to motivate yourself to study and in which you find it hard. Talk about why you chose the subjects you did and the reasons why you want to do well in each of them.

Each carry out a daily review of your time, then discuss together what you learnt from it about how you use your time. Identify any time-wasting events and decide what you could do to cut them out.

When you start doing GCSE or Standard Grade courses, you will almost certainly find that you are having to spend more time studying. It is very important, therefore, to develop time-management techniques that will not only enable you to succeed in your work, but will also enable you to have time for leisure.

GET MOTIVATED

A key factor in whether or not you make the best use of your time is how motivated you are. The chances are that, like most people, you find it easier to get down to work in some subjects – the ones you are good at, interested in and enjoy doing – than in other subjects – the ones you have chosen because you know you need to get a qualification in them, even though you find them less interesting. Therefore, it is important to remember what your reasons are for wanting to do well in a particular subject and why it is important for you to work hard at it. If you are going to use your time effectively, then it is essential that you adopt the right attitude to your courses. The more motivated you are, the more you will be prepared to find time for your studies and to make any sacrifices that may be necessary in order for you to succeed in your examinations.

REVIEW HOW YOU USE YOUR TIME

It is worth reviewing your use of time to see if you are using it as efficiently as you could be. One way of doing this is to carry out a daily review. In the evening, just before you go to bed, draw up a chart showing each 15 minute interval throughout the day, and fill in exactly how you spent your time. Then, analyse your use of time, trying to identify periods in which you might have used the time more productively.

Try to identify time-wasting events, such as:

- time spent chatting at school when you should have been doing private study;
- too much time spent watching TV;
- unnecessarily long telephone calls;
- unproductive time spent waiting or travelling;
- time spent searching for books and equipment to enable you to start studying.

Once you have identified any time-wasting events, you need to think of a plan of action that will enable you to eliminate them in the future. For example, you may have to set a time-limit on the length of your telephone calls or to cut down on the amount of TV you allow yourself to watch.

It may also be necessary for you to review your lifestyle completely and to consider whether you have got the right balance between study time and leisure time. You may come to the conclusion that you will have to cut down the number of activities you are involved in or the number of evenings you go out each week. You may be faced with some hard choices. It is not easy to have to reduce the amount of time you spend on an activity which you really enjoy, in order to concentrate on your studies. But you need to consider what your long-term goals are, and how much success in your exams really matters to you.

Plan ahead

You should have already developed the habits of keeping a homework diary and planning your evenings so that you can fit your homework in. Since you will now have coursework projects that sometimes last for a period of several weeks, you will need to start planning even further ahead. Write key dates in a diary or on a calendar and consider drawing up a timetable at the beginning of each week. Planning ahead enables you to see whether you are allowing enough time for studying, and to decide in advance whether there are any activities you will have to cut out.

SET TARGETS

It is important, when planning and organising your use of time, to set yourself realistic targets. Try to break down large assignments into a number of shorter, more manageable tasks. Then, set yourself short-term targets. By doing so, you will be able to show yourself that you are gradually making progress, and avoid getting stressed because you are worried that you won't finish the whole assignment in time.

ORGANISE YOUR WORK SPACE

To ensure that you get as much work as possible done in the time you have set aside for studying, you need to have a study area that is kept organised and free from distractions. Get in the habit of tidying away books and equipment at the end of each study session. It will stop the worktop from getting cluttered, and enable you to find things quickly the next time you need them.

	morning	afternoon	evening
Mon 6th	school	school / TV	study
Tue 7th	school	school / study	swimming
Wed 8th	school	school / study	meet Sue + Dave
Thu. 9th	school	school / trumpet	Youth club
Fri 10th	school	school / football	study
Sat 11th	study	shopping	cinema
Sun 12th	TV	study	study

ON YOUR OWN

Each draw up a study timetable for next week. Start by listing all the family, social and leisure commitments you have. Put them on your timetable and fill in the times when you plan to eat and to watch TV. Then, fill in the times when you plan to do your studying.

IN PAIRS

Show your timetables to each other, and discuss whether you have enough time for studying. Discuss which activities you could cut out, if there is not enough study time.

Discuss where you do your studying. Do you always do it in the same place or do you do it in different places? Do you like to have complete silence when you are studying or do you like listening to music? When do you find you work best – in the morning or in the evening, or can you work equally well at different times of the day?

Work together and design what you consider to be an ideal study space for a person of your age. Make a list of all its features. Then, compare your ideal study space with the place where you actually do most of your studying. Is there anything you could do to your study place to make it more suitable for your needs?

GETTING DOWN TO WORK

It is important to make the best use of your time when getting down to work. Below are five ways to help you achieve this.

1 Develop a routine

Different people study in different ways. Some people prefer to get straight down to work as soon as they get in from school, while others prefer to relax and unwind for an hour before getting started. Some people do different things on different days, depending on their other commitments. If you can, it is a good idea to get into a routine, even if you have to have different routines for different days of the week. You will find it easier to get down to work if there is a pattern to your studying.

2 Identify priorities

Because you are studying a range of different subjects, you will often have several different pieces of work to do. It is necessary, therefore, to think carefully about which pieces of work you need to do first, and to establish an order of priorities. Think about how long each piece of work will take, when it is due in, and how important and urgent it is. List the pieces of work in order of priority, starting with the one that is most important and urgent and ending with the one that is least important and not urgent. Then, do the pieces of work in that order. This will help you to avoid having to rush pieces of work because you spent time on less urgent tasks, and will help you to meet your deadlines.

3 Use short periods of spare time

Often, in the evenings or at the weekend, you will find that you have an extra twenty minutes or so of spare time, perhaps because you got home earlier than expected or you are waiting for someone or something. Try to use these short periods of time constructively – for example, by reading another chapter of the novel you are studying or learning some vocabulary. The more you make use of your spare time in this way, the easier you will find it to get all your studying done and to have enough time for your social life and leisure activities.

4 Don't allow yourself to be distracted or interrupted

Once you have started studying, don't allow family or friends to distract you or to interrupt you. Get into the habit of saying 'No' if someone in your family keeps pestering you to do something with them or keeps on urging you to come and watch something on TV. Similarly, if someone rings you up while you are studying, explain to them that you are busy and that you will ring them back as soon as you have finished. Dealing with interruptions can be very difficult if the person who is interrupting you does not think studying is as important as you think it is, so be prepared to be assertive. After all, it is your future that may be at stake if you do not study hard enough, not theirs.

5 Give yourself breaks

In order to study effectively, you need to give yourself regular breaks. When you first start a piece of work, your concentration level is high. However, after a while your level of concentration will start to drop. Once the end of a piece of work is in sight, your concentration level goes up slightly.

Level of concentration

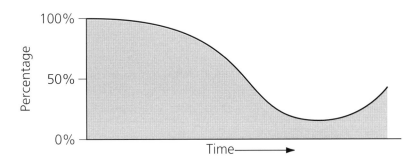

It is a good idea, therefore, to give yourself regular breaks. If you give yourself a break of say 5 or 10 minutes between each half-hour or three-quarters of an hour's study, then you will work more effectively. You will keep your concentration levels high, because you return to work refreshed each time you have had a short break.

Level of concentration

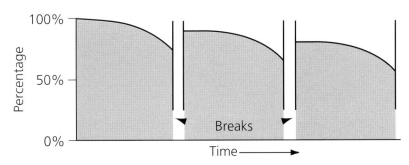

Working at home

Dear Gita
My problem is my parents. They keep interfering. First of all, they want to know what I've got to do. Then, they keep coming and interrupting, so I can't concentrate properly. Then, when I don't get good marks, they start going on at me.

Alana

Dear Gita
My problem is that I have a lot of trouble getting down to work. I'm always getting told off because my work isn't in on time, but there's so much of it,
I never know where to start and I spend a lot of time worrying about getting low marks. It's really getting me down.

Tamar

IN PAIRS

Study Alana's and Tamar's letters, and draft replies to them. Then, share the replies you have written in a class discussion.

ROLE PLAY

Role play a scene in which a young person of your age gets interrupted while they are trying to study. Do the scene several times, showing different ways of dealing with the interruption and taking it in turns to be the young person.

IN GROUPS

Discuss the kinds of problems you face when trying to get down to work at home. Suggest ways of trying to cope with these difficulties.

Prepare a group statement about the difficulties of studying at home, and how to deal with them. Then, share your ideas in a class discussion.

2 Coursework projects

Tackling coursework

Many courses require you to complete coursework assignments and projects. Sometimes the coursework will be set by your teacher. For example, in History you may be presented with certain pieces of historical evidence and asked to interpret them by writing an empathy assignment, in which you present an issue or a series of events from a particular point of view. In Technology you may be presented with a problem and required to design a solution for it.

Often, you will be given a certain amount of individual choice, so that you can select a topic that interests you. For example, in Geography you may be asked to plan an enquiry on a topic that you choose. As part of a vocational course, you may have to select a particular business or industry and find out how it is structured and organised.

IDENTIFYING THE AIM

Before you begin work on any assignment or project, you need to understand clearly what you are required to do. The two key questions you need to ask are:
- What is the aim of the assignment?
- What skills and abilities does the assignment require me to show?

If you are unsure about the purpose of the assignment or the skills you have got to demonstrate, then either talk to your teacher or look at the course syllabus.

The nature of the coursework will vary from subject to subject, but if you are carrying out an investigation, the four basic skills you will be required to show are:

1 **Planning skills**
   The ability to identify a problem or question and to choose appropriate methods of investigating it.

2 **Research skills**
   The ability to identify sources of information and to collect data.

3 **Interpretation and evaluation skills**
   The ability to interpret the data you collect, to evaluate it and to draw conclusions from it.

4 **Reporting skills**
   The ability to communicate your findings in a logical, orderly way.

●● IN PAIRS ●●

Discuss any GCSE assignments and projects which you are currently doing. Say what the purpose of each assignment is and what skills and abilities each assignment is designed to test.

Imagine that as part of a General Studies GCSE you are required to do a coursework assignment on an environmental issue. Choose an environmental issue, identify a problem or question and decide on the methods you would use to investigate it.

Conducting enquiries

There are six stages or processes that you need to go through when you are conducting an enquiry. Follow these whenever you are carrying out an investigation.

1 Identify the problem or question.

2 Select appropriate methods of investigating it.

3 Collect relevant data.

4 Analyse the data.

5 Evaluate the data.

6 Report your findings and conclusions.

IDENTIFYING INFORMATION SOURCES

Once you have identified the problem or question you are going to investigate, the next step is to ask yourself: where can I find the information I need? There are two main types of data – primary data and secondary data. Primary data is information which you obtain by measuring, observing and questioning. Secondary data is information which you obtain by reading and studying what other people have written and recorded. Secondary data sources include books and articles, photographs, videos, tapes and CD Roms.

The chart gives details of the main sources of information that you can use.

•• IN PAIRS ••

Study the chart. Discuss which sources provide primary data and which sources provide secondary data.

Choose a GCSE project that you are currently working on and take it in turns to tell each other the sources you plan to use to provide you with the data you require. Look again at the chart, and see if there are any further sources of information you or your partner might use.

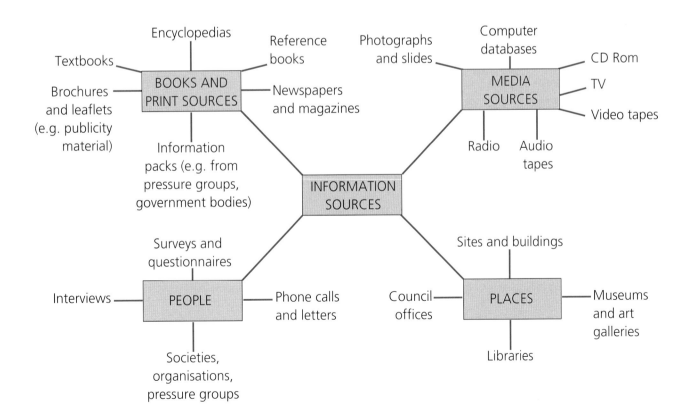

FINDING INFORMATION

USING LIBRARIES

Libraries have two main uses as sources of information for your coursework:

1 For finding other people's work on your subject, including their views.

2 For obtaining other people's primary data (census data, planning documents etc.).

You should not only use your school library, but also your local library as it can offer you a wider range of information. As well as borrowing books from the library, you can consult their reference section. Libraries have indexes, often computerised, which list all of their books. On the index, you can look for a particular book, or for books by a particular author, or you can simply look up a subject area to find out what books the library has on that subject.

Libraries usually have periodicals, newspapers, computer disks and CD Roms which can be consulted for more information. They normally have past copies of newspapers on microfilm or CD Rom.

Local information, such as any planning documents, maps and photographic records, is also available in libraries.

It is always a good idea to ask the librarian if there is any information on the subject you are researching that you have missed, because the library may hold information that you are not aware of.

ON YOUR OWN

Study the advice on using libraries. Make a list of all the different types of information sources that you can find in libraries in addition to books.

USING IT

Often, the quickest way to locate and retrieve information for your coursework will be by using computer technology. The following examples show some of the ways you can use computers to help you to find information.

Rebecca used a CD Rom and the library's computerised index system to provide her with information for her RE investigation into Jewish religious festivals.

A CD Rom is a compact disc which stores text, graphics and sound. The amount of information that can be stored is equivalent to around 200,000 pages of typed text. So one CD Rom can store an entire set of encyclopedias.

Rebecca inserted a CD Rom with a set of encyclopedias on it into the computer and searched for the entry under *Judaism*. She then scanned the entry to find the section on Jewish religious festivals. When she found it, she downloaded the section onto a floppy disc on which she was storing information for her project, so that she could study it later. She then went across to a computer terminal in order to use the library's computerised index to find out whether there were any books or articles in the resources centre which might contain information on Jewish religious festivals. She typed in the keyword *Judaism* and found that in addition to a number of books, there was also a resource pack and a video tape. She noted down the details, and then went to see if they were on the shelves.

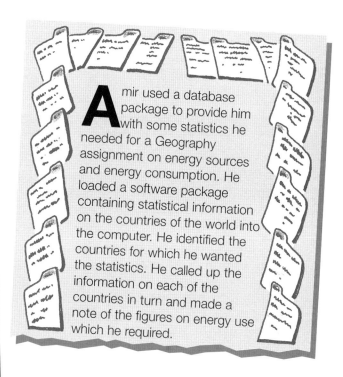

Trevor used a documents package in order to locate and retrieve the documents he needed to study for his historical enquiry into the establishment of the welfare state. He loaded a piece of software containing important texts relating to Britain from 1939 to 1989. He typed in *welfare state* and the computer immediately located a large number of references. He scanned the list to find those that related to the period during and immediately after the Second World War. Once he had identified the texts which referred to the period he was studying, he printed them out. He then sorted them into chronological order and put them in his History file so that he could study them in detail later.

Amir used a database package to provide him with some statistics he needed for a Geography assignment on energy sources and energy consumption. He loaded a software package containing statistical information on the countries of the world into the computer. He identified the countries for which he wanted the statistics. He called up the information on each of the countries in turn and made a note of the figures on energy use which he required.

Jason is using the Internet in order to search for information for his RE assignment. He has been researching Indian religious sects and has discovered that there is a sect called the Jains. He has used a CD with a set of encyclopedias on it, and has found an article about the Jains, which he has printed out. Neither his school library, nor his local library have been able to provide him with any books on the

subject. However, he has been given the Internet address of an American library which specialises in books on religion and religious sects. He decides to contact them via the Internet. He accesses the library's main index on the Internet through a computer modem, and begins his search. The Internet is a worldwide network of computers into which organisations and individuals can place information which can be accessed by others. It contains information and ideas on every kind of subject. Each user has an address for identification. Through the Internet you can join a discussion group of other users interested in your subject, and even have real-time conversations with them. The Internet has over 30 million users and is growing rapidly.

● **ON YOUR OWN** ●

Practise using your computer skills to locate and retrieve information.

1 Choose a topic you are studying in one of your subjects.

2 Use a computerised index in either the resources centre or a local library to search for books on the topic.

3 Use a CD Rom with a set of encyclopedias on it to find a useful article on the topic and either download it onto a floppy disc or print it out.

4 See if you can locate a software package e.g. a database program which contains information about the topic. Search through the program, locate the information and print it out.

5 Use the Internet to locate a list of titles of books on the topic.

INTERVIEWS, QUESTIONNAIRES AND SURVEYS

Sometimes you will want to collect primary data. This can be done by observation, issuing a questionnaire or holding interviews. The method you use will depend on what data you want to collect.

Interviews

Interviews are a useful way of collecting information, particularly if you want to find out opinions and attitudes as well as facts.

Before the interview

- Decide who you need to interview and what you want to discover from the interview. In some cases, you might want to interview someone because they are an expert on the topic you are investigating. In other cases, you might want to interview someone because they hold a particular point of view.

- Make a list of the questions you want to ask and work out how long you will need for the interview.

- Contact the person you wish to interview and arrange an appointment. Be sure to explain what your project is and why you want to interview them.

During the interview

- Either take notes or make a tape recording. If you want to tape record the interview, check that the person does not mind.

- Make sure you cover all your prepared questions, but be ready to pick up points that arise during the interview and are relevant, and explore them by asking further questions.

- Stop at regular intervals to summarise what the person has said in order to make sure that you have understood them.

After the interview

- Find time as soon as possible to write up the interview.

- Be selective. Analyse what was said and pick out the key points. Don't try to write out the interview in full.

Questionnaires

If you want to collect information from a lot of people, then the best way of doing so is to use a questionnaire. Questionnaires enable you to investigate patterns of behaviour and to compare people's views. Often, they can provide you with data that can be presented in statistical form using graphs, charts and tables.

PREPARING A QUESTIONNAIRE

When you are preparing a questionnaire, you need to think carefully about the questions you ask. The questions can be either *closed* or *open*. A closed question restricts the answer to one of those given on the questionnaire:

e.g.

> **How often do you go to the cinema?**
> One or more times a week ☐
> once a fortnight ☐
> once a month ☐
> two or three times a year ☐
> less than once a year ☐

An open question is one that does not restrict the answer that can be given:

e.g.

> **What do you think is the main cause of vandalism on the estate?**

The questions you ask must be clear and unambiguous. You also need to guard against asking them in such a way that you influence the answers.

You will also have to decide who you are going to ask to complete your questionnaire. There are two basic types of sample:

1 A representative sample in which you try to get views from a cross-section of people, by giving the questionnaire to an equal proportion of men and women, people of different ages, backgrounds etc.

2 A random sample in which you randomly pick as many people as you want to answer the questionnaire, without worrying about such things as their sex, age or background.

Study the ideas for questions that Tracy has jotted down for a survey of the use of public transport by people living on the Lee Vale Estate, and design a questionnaire to find out the information she needs.

Survey of public transport use by residents of Lee Vale Estate
- When you go into the centre of Croxby how do you normally travel?
- How often do you use the bus service?
- Do you think the bus service is better than it used to be?
- What changes/improvements would you like to see to public transport for the estate?

Compare your questionnaire with those other people have produced, and use the questionnaire checklist to suggest ways of improving them.

QUESTIONNAIRE DESIGN CHECKLIST

- Does it have a clear purpose?
- Does it explain the purpose to the people who are being questioned?
- Does it record the name and date of the interviewer?
- Does it ask for sufficient details about the person being questioned?
- Are the questions clear and unambiguous?
- Does it avoid 'loaded' questions? e.g. By asking: 'Do you think the environment needs improving and if so how? rather than 'What could be done to improve the environment?'
- Are all the questions relevant to the purpose of the questionnaire?
- Will the questions provide all the information required? Are there any other key questions that could have been included?
- Is the questionnaire easy to fill in? Could the layout be improved in any way?

Data Collection

The following article gives details of the information sources used by one student for his GCSE Geography enquiry. Michael Evans decided to study the village of Llay near Wrexham. He investigated why, after the closure of a coal mine in 1966, the village has continued to thrive and grow.

Data Collection

Michael carried out a door-to-door survey of a hundred and fifty households, asking people about their jobs, where they worked, how long they had lived in Llay and whether they had any specific reason for doing so.

He also collected information on Llay Industrial Estate, visiting firms there and asking about the number of people they employed, how many of their employees lived in Llay and why the firm chose Llay Estate for their premises.

Personal interviews were also carried out. The most valuable one was with the former Llay Main miner, Mr E H Evans, who had lived in Llay for almost sixty years. Michael used maps from the County Surveyor's office and County Council, and wrote letters asking for information from the Coal Board, Brymbo Steel Works, Shotton Steel Works, and Sharp, about people working for them in Llay. He visited the local library for information on the history of the village and the colliery, and carried out an environmental survey to evaluate the local environment. Michael wrote up his results in four chapters: population, housing, employment and internal comparisons.

Study the article 'Data Collection' and talk about the sources of information which Michael Evans used in order to collect data for his project.

ANALYSING DATA

Once you have collected all your data, the next step is to analyse it. For her GCSE Geography enquiry, Sharon used a questionnaire to investigate the views of the people of Churchdown, a village seven miles from Gloucester, on whether Churchdown railway station should be reopened. Over 1000 residents had petitioned the local councils saying that they would use the station regularly if it was reopened. The councils said it would cost £200,000 to reopen it and that they could not find that amount of money.

Sharon asked people whether or not they thought the station should be reopened, what reasons people had for wanting it reopened, whether or not they would use the station and, if so, how frequently. She also asked their views on the only other form of public transport available in Churchdown – the local bus service.

Once the questionnaires were completed, Sharon collated her data and drew a number of charts and graphs, which she then analysed.

A pie chart to show whether or not residents wanted the station re–opened.

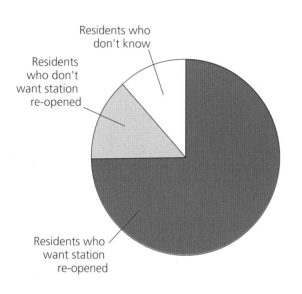

Reasons stated for re–opening the station.

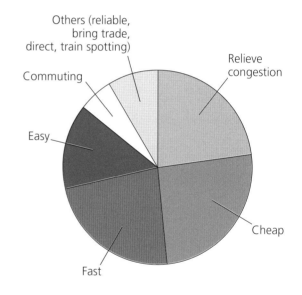

Uses of the station: what people said.

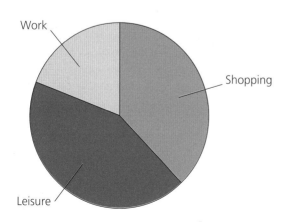

How often would you use the station?

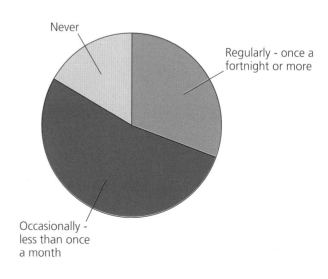

Is the bus service reliable?

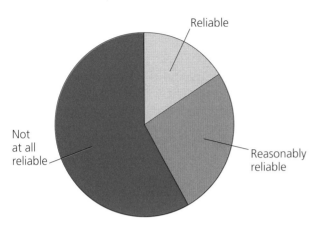

Study Sharon's charts and graphs and discuss what conclusions she could draw from them about who was most in favour of reopening the station, about what people saw as the main benefits of reopening it, why they would use it and how often they would use it. Do you think her findings supported the arguments of those people who were petitioning for the reopening of Churchdown station? Give your reasons. (Note: Sharon interviewed 50 people. She thought it rather a small sample and felt that to get more valid conclusions she would need to interview many more people.)

WRITING UP

Whether you are using a word processor or writing by hand, your writing up should always be done in five stages:

Stage 1 Making a plan.

Stage 2 Writing a first draft.

Stage 3 Redrafting and altering the text until you are satisfied with it.

Stage 4 Writing your final draft.

Stage 5 Checking for spelling and punctuation errors.

PLANNING AND STRUCTURING COURSEWORK REPORTS

A report of an investigation should contain the following sections:

1 **Title page**

A simple statement of the issue or question you investigated.

2 **Contents page**

A list of the various sections of the report, stating the number of the page or paragraph in which each section appears.

3 **Introduction**

An explanation of the aims of the investigation and of the methods used. You should explain why you decided to tackle the investigation in the way you did and outline any problems you encountered in collecting the data you required.

4 **Main body**

Full details of the data you collected and your analysis and evaluation of it. The main body is the core of your report and should be presented in a logical, orderly sequence, with the different ideas and items of information grouped in separate sections or paragraphs. It is often helpful to show these divisions by using headings and sub-headings and numbering the various sections. Where appropriate, present data in the form of tables, graphs and diagrams and make clear reference to such data in your text.

5 **Conclusion**

A brief summary of the main findings of the investigation. Refer to the aim of the assignment, stating whether you achieved your purpose, and whether there are any questions that remain unanswered or new ones that have arisen. Outline any further research which could be done to provide more information.

6 **Sources**

A list of all the sources you have used in the preparation of your report.

Note – Between the conclusion and the sources, you may also want to include an appendix, or a number of appendices, consisting, for example, of detailed data that it would be inappropriate to include in the main body of the report e.g. samples of questionnaire responses, or the full text of a key article which you have referred to several times in the main body of the report.

3 Developing your reading skills

When you are reading, the technique you use will depend on the purpose of your reading. Often, when you are studying for exams, you will want a detailed understanding of a passage or chapter, so you will need to read the text closely. A useful technique for detailed reading is the method known as SQ3R (skim, question, read, recall review).

Using the SQ3R technique

STEP 1 – Survey

Aim: To get a general impression of what information the passage or chapter contains and how it is presented.

Method:

- Glance through the passage or chapter looking at headings and sub-headings, pictures and diagrams.

- Skim read the whole passage or chapter to try to get an idea of how it is structured. Be on the lookout for clues in the introduction and in the summary or conclusion that will help to tell you how the passage develops.

STEP 2 – Question

Aim: To define precisely what information you want to obtain from reading this particular text.

Method:

- Ask yourself questions about the topic you are studying and the text you are about to read. For example: What do I know about this topic? What do I need to find out? What exactly is this text about? What do I hope to learn from this passage?

- Write down the specific questions that you hope the passage will answer.

STEP 3 – Read

Aim: To understand the passage and to find the answers to your questions.

Method:

- Read the passage closely, pausing to study any graphs, diagrams or charts whenever you are directed to do so, and to look up words you don't understand in the glossary or a dictionary.

- At this stage, do not interrupt your reading by trying to make notes. However, if it is your own book or worksheet, you could use a pencil or highlighter pen to mark key points.

STEP 4 – Recall

Aim: To check that you have found out the answers to your questions and that you have fully understood the passage.

Method:

- Think about what the passage says. What are its key points? Does it answer your questions? Which sections is it worth making notes on?

- Re-read the passage, making notes on the sections that answer your questions and working carefully through any difficult parts.

STEP 5 – Review

Aim: To ensure that you will be able to remember what you have learned from your reading.

Method:

- Check through your notes to make sure that you can understand them, then file them together with all your other notes on that topic.

- Tell someone else in your group what you learned from your reading or show them your notes and ask them to test you.

Farming the sea

On the whole, humans are still hunters as far as sea life is concerned. You can get 'farmed fish', but fencing the sea isn't as easy as fencing the land. It is easier if the land has long narrow inlets. So, many fish farms are found in Scotland and Norway. It costs a lot of money to farm fish, so only those that have a high price in the shops, like salmon or lobsters, are farmed.

Fish farms can cause problems. The fish may have to be given chemicals to keep them healthy in unnatural surroundings, or growth hormone so that they grow more quickly. These chemicals can pollute the surrounding sea. Good fish farming doesn't use chemicals.

Of course, shellfish have been farmed for many hundreds of years. They stay where they are put, which makes things a lot easier!

The main problem with sea fishing is that we are getting too good at it. Modern techniques include:

- Factory ships which can freeze and process the catch at sea. The small fishing boats don't have to keep returning to port every two weeks or so, but off-load their catch onto the factory vessel.

- Sonar sound which is used to detect shoals of fish deep under water that would otherwise escape.

- Drift nets up to 30 kilometres long, which hang down into the sea. They catch everything, and kill it, so unwanted fish can't be thrown back into the sea. These nets have damaged the ecosystem so much in many fishing areas that they have now been banned.

All this has resulted in overfishing. This means that there is a strong danger that the population of a fish species gets so small that it is unable to reproduce. For fish, reproduction is a very hit-and-miss affair. The female lays eggs in shallow water, and the male squirts sperm all over them – if he can find them. As more and more adult fish are caught there aren't enough left to breed.

The graph shows the effect of overfishing mackerel in the seas near Britain. Fewer and fewer fish are caught each year. This isn't helped by the fact that European countries have been using the North Sea for waste disposal for so long. Many of the fish that are caught are unhealthy, due to the chemical pollution from large rivers such as the Rhine.

•• IN PAIRS ••

Each use the SQ3R method to read the passage (left) about farming the sea. Then, tell each other what you learned from the passage. Discuss the questions you framed before your detailed reading, and show each other the notes you made. Whose reading was more effective? Why?

Practise using the SQ3R method when you are given reading assignments. Afterwards, compare your questions and notes, test each other about what you learned, and discuss any problems you encountered in your reading.

Catch of mackerel in UK waters

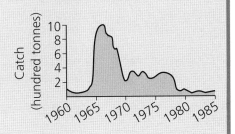

MAKING A SUMMARY

Making a summary is one of the skills that you need to develop during your GCSE courses. For a reading assignment, you may be asked to read a passage or a chapter and to write a summary of it. If you are asked to write a summary, use the SQ3R method and do not start writing the summary until you reach the recall stage.

ON YOUR OWN

Prepare a summary of the article on superstores. Use the SQ3R method and try to make your summary about half the length of the article.

IN GROUPS

Show each other your summaries. Talk about which parts of the article you omitted and why. Discuss whose summary is the best and why.

Five rules for summarising

1 Leave out anything that is trivial and unimportant.

2 Leave out any material that is redundant. 'Redundant material' is anything that is not essential, e.g. details, examples, repetitions or comments.

3 Look for ways of combining lists or groups of items.

4 Look for topic sentences. A topic sentence is one which either introduces or sums up the information contained in a section or paragraph.

5 If a paragraph has no topic sentence, make one up.

The growth of the superstore

Most people will be familiar with the crowded conditions of many city centre shopping areas and the difficulty of carrying cumbersome bags of shopping to the bus stop or car park – if parking is available, that is! At certain times road traffic can get extremely congested and this adds to the problems of shopping. Companies find the costs of land, as well as the rent and rates in central areas very high. Sometimes all these problems outweigh the advantages of being located at the city centre, with its many potential customers. As a result, firms have moved to completely new locations in the suburbs or on the fringes of cities, and built very much larger shops, known as superstores.

A superstore has been defined as having at least 25000 square feet (2367sq.m.) of sales area. This means it is much bigger than the average supermarket. Some superstores are even bigger than this because they carry many non-food lines such as gardening and do-it-yourself items. The advantages for the customer are that superstores are spacious with wide shopping aisles, have rows of check-out points, and, above all, they have huge car parks. People travel to them from long distances and do a lot of their shopping in one go. (This is apart from regular items bought from small local shops, and major items which are bought infrequently, such as furniture or clothes.) Because most people travel to the superstore by car once or twice a week, and get most of their needs there, this is sometimes known as 'one-stop shopping'.

Not everyone has benefitted from the growth of superstores. People without cars can find access to the superstores very difficult. However, in certain areas, large stores, such as Tescos, have made arrangements for special buses to carry people to and from their stores from nearby towns and villages on a regular basis. Superstores need plenty of staff and so provide jobs, but they have also led to loss of trade or closure of small independent shops in the older shopping areas.

INTERPRETING EVIDENCE

When you are studying evidence, in subjects such as history, you have to develop the skill of interpreting texts in order to understand how events or facts are being presented from a particular viewpoint.

●● **IN PAIRS** ●●

Study the three texts about the development of the railways in England during the 1820s and 1830s. Discuss what you learn from them about a) how the Railway Company tried to convince people that the building of the railways would be beneficial b) why some people were opposed to the building of the first railways c) how people felt about travelling on the railway for the first time. Then, discuss the point of view from which each extract is written and how this affects your view of them as evidence.

As well as the transport of goods between Liverpool and Manchester, a good deal of revenue may be expected from the rich mines near St Helens. These coals at present pass along the Sankey Canal and down the Mersey to Liverpool, a distance of about 30 miles. By the railway, the distance will be shortened by one half and the charge for transport very much reduced.

(from the Prospectus of the Liverpool and Manchester Rail-Road Company, 1824)

We have sad work with Lord Derby, Lord Sefton and Bradshaw, the great canal proprietor, whose grounds we go through with the planned railway. Their ground is blockaded on every side to prevent us getting on with the survey. Bradshaw fired guns through his grounds in the course of the night, to prevent the surveyor coming on in the dark. We are to have a grand field-day next week. The Liverpool Railway people are determined to force a survey through if possible.

(George Stephenson, the railway developer, writing to a friend in 1824 about surveying the route for the Liverpool to Manchester railway.)

We had two seats in the Mail part of the train, thinking it would be easier than our own carriage, which was lashed on to a machine behind, and in which we sent the servants. Luckily, Merthyr and I had the four places in our division to ourselves, and no strangers came in to annoy us. The thirty-six miles took exactly an hour and a half. My mamma had entreated that I should not go by this conveyance, lest some accident should befall. It would have taken us about four hours to make the journey with post horses, and the temptation of saving so much time and fatigue was not to be resisted. I never had a pleasanter journey. It is much smoother and easier than a carriage, and the sensation cannot alarm, by reason of its steadiness. My introduction to the Railway is a memorable event in my life.

(from the Diary of Lady Charlotte Guest, November 3rd 1833)

4 Notes and note-making

Whatever subject you are studying, it is important to keep notes that you can use for revision before the examinations.

The type of notes you make will depend on the topic you are studying and your own personal note-making style. Some students prefer to make blocks of notes, using numbers, headings and sub-headings. Others prefer to make notes in the form of diagrams. Since your notes are a personal learning aid, it is up to you to find the note-making style that suits you. Whichever style you use, the most important thing is to make notes that are neat, clear and easy for you to understand.

Always make sure you include all the main points, but without unnecessary detail. Events should be listed rather than described. It is also helpful to use abbreviations and signs. If, when you revise, you can't remember what some of your notes refer to, then you need to refresh your memory by looking in the textbook.

•• IN PAIRS ••

Simon and Aloyna both used the same source for their notes on methods for preserving food. Study the two different types of notes. Which set of notes do you find easier to understand? Which set of notes would you find it easier to revise from?

Block notes
Preserving Food   Aloyna
Prevents disease. Keeps food fresh. Kills or makes inactive bacteria and fungi.
1. Sterilisation
  - Bacteria killed by high temp.
  - Food sealed in air-tight containers.
  - Preserved for a long time.
2. Pasteurisation (cheese, milk)
  - Flash heat milk to 75°C
  - Some bacteria survive, ∴ must be kept in fridge.
3. Refrigeration (below 5°C)
  - Stops bacteria reproducing but they restart when food warms up.
4. Freezing (-18°C to -24°C)
  - Stops all bacterial activity
5. Drying (vegetables, fruit, some meats)
  - Bacteria can't reproduce without water.
  Note: freeze drying of custard powder, soups. Freeze, then draw off ice.
6. Chemical preservatives (sulphur dioxide, nitrates, nitrites)
  - Stops growth or kills bacteria.
  - E numbers.
7. Irradiation (γ-radiation)
  - Kills bacteria + moulds
  - Doesn't affect enzymes + ripening.
Note: Food can't be sold for 24 hrs.

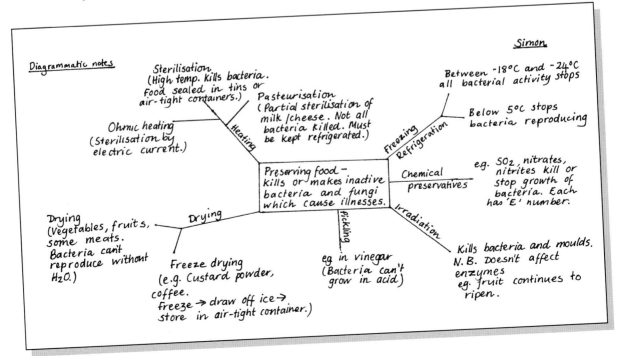

••• 22 •••

Immunisation

Immunisation, or vaccination, promotes active immunity to disease-causing microorganisms. It involves being injected with or swallowing a substance called a vaccine.

Vaccines are made from one of the following:

- Dead microorganisms, e.g. whooping-cough vaccine is made from dead bacteria.
- A weakened form of microorganism which is harmless. Vaccines made like this are called attenuated vaccines, e.g. the vaccine against tuberculosis and sabin oral vaccine (the vaccine against poliomyelitis).
- A substance from the microorganism which does not cause the disease, e.g. diptheria vaccine.

What effect does a vaccine have?

Antigens from the dead or attenuated microorganisms in the vaccine stimulate the lymphocytes to produce antibodies. So, when the same active, harmful microorganisms invade the body, the antibodies made in response to the vaccine destroy them.

The active immunity produced by vaccines can protect a person from disease for a long time, although booster vaccines may be needed. Booster vaccines are weaker than the first vaccine and are used to keep the person's body producing the antibodies that they need to maintain their immunity. Children in the UK are immunised against six diseases which used to cause many deaths. They are diphtheria, tetanus, whooping cough, poliomyelitis, tuberculosis and German measles.

ON YOUR OWN

Study the passage on immunisation, which is taken from a GCSE science textbook, and make notes which answer the following questions:

- What is immunisation?
- Which diseases has immunisation helped to control?
- What is a vaccine and how are vaccines made?
- What is the difference between active immunity and passive immunity?

IN GROUPS

Compare the notes you have made on immunisation. Discuss whose notes contain all the essential information and are clear and easy to understand.

Passive Immunity

Not all vaccines contain antigens which stimulate the body to produce antibodies. Instead, some contain antibodies that come from other animals. For example, anti-tetanus vaccine contains anti-tetanus antibodies produced by horses. Immunity which comes from antibodies made in another animal is called passive immunity.

Although it is short-lived, passive immunity is important for babies. While they are breast-feeding, babies recieve antibodies from their mother's milk which protect them from disease-causing microorganisms. By the time this protection wears off, the baby is able to make its own antibodies.

DEVELOPING YOUR NOTE-MAKING SKILLS

Skilled note-takers save time by using a number of different types of abbreviations.

1 Common short forms of words:
   Tues for Tuesday; Dec for December; st for street; Col for Colonel.

2 Common acronyms (an acronym is a word formed from the initial letters of a group of words):
   UN for United Nations; TUC for Trades Union Congress; BBC for British Broadcasting Corporation.

3 Common Latin abbreviations:
   pm (post meridiem) = after noon; p.a. (per annum) = each year; e.g. (exempli gratia) = for example.

4 Widely understood symbols and punctuation marks:
   $\therefore$ + $\rightarrow$?

5 Using only the first part/syllable of a word:
   diff; intro; av; Parl; nat; usu; prob.

6 Writing the first syllable and last letter of a word:
   govt; advs; disadvs; fams.

7 Missing out some or all of the letters:
   frst brn; prblms; e'quake; revn.

   Here are some notes Damian made on Britain's electoral system:

●●   IN PAIRS   ●●

Study Damian's notes, and discuss all the different types of abbreviations that he uses.

1. <u>General elections</u> must be held once every 5 yrs. PM calls gen. election. May be forced to resign if govt. loses confidence vote in Parl.

2. UK divided into <u>constituencies</u> in England, in Wales, in Scot, in NI.

3. <u>Candidates</u> must be 21+. Puts down deposit of £500. Loses deposit if gets less than 5% of vote.

4. <u>Voting</u> by secret ballot. Reformers (e.g. Lib Dems) want P.R. Voters must be 18+. One man one vote intro. 1884. Votes for women over 30 intro. 1918 + for all adult women 1928.

Table A: Common Latin abbreviations

ABBREVIATION	MEANING
AD	Anno Domini/after the birth of Christ
ad inf	ad infinitum/for ever
App	Appendix/supplement
cf	compare with
cl	centilitre
cm	centimetre
etc	etcetera/and so on
et al	and others
et seq	and following
ie	id est/that is to say
ibid	the same again
kg	kilogramme
kHz	kilohertz
m	metre
pa	per annum/each year
No	Numero/number
non seq	that does not follow
pp	per pro/for
pro tem	for the time being
viz	namely

Table B: Widely used symbols and punctuation

SYMBOL	MEANING
$\therefore$	therefore, so
$\because$	because
&	and
+	plus, add, and
–	take away, minus, subtract
x	times, multiplied by, kiss
$\div$	divided by
=	equals, is the same as
$\neq$	does not equal, is not the same as
$\simeq$	roughly equal, nearly the same as
?	question, query, don't know
!	exclamation, surprise
> ≫	is greater than, much greater than
< ≪	is less than, much less than
$\propto$	is proportionate to
$\not\propto$	is not proportionate to
%	percentage
*	special note
✕	delete, take out, wrong
⌐	add, inset

Recording your sources

It is important not only to make notes of the information you collect, but also to record the source of the information. When you take notes from a book, always write down the following details:

- the title of the book
- the name of the author
- the name of the publisher
- the date of publication
- the number(s) of the page(s) where you found the information

This will enable you to quote your sources accurately in your report and, if necessary, to find the information again if you need to check any of the details.

Similarly, always note the details of other sources. For example, when you print out text from a computer, make sure that the copy contains details of the source. If you make a photocopy of an article from a newspaper or magazine, note the title of the publication and the date of the issue.

IN PAIRS

Study Table A – Common Latin abbreviations. Pick out the ones you know. Then try to learn the ones you don't know and take it in turns to test each other.

Study Table B – Widely used symbols and punctuation marks. Talk about the ones you already use in your notes and others which you think it would be useful to start using.

IN PAIRS

How conscientious are you about recording your sources? Show each other the notes you are making for one of your coursework projects and talk about how good you are at recording your sources and why it is important to do so.

5 Developing your writing skills

WRITING ESSAYS

For your GCSE or Standard Grade courses, you will have to write essays as part of your coursework and in your examinations. The types of essays you have to write will vary from subject to subject.

In English you will have to write a range of different types of essays. You may be asked to write an autobiographical essay, describing a personal experience, or to write a discursive essay on a particular topic, exploring different points of view and giving your own personal views and opinions. You may also have to write a factual essay on a subject that you have researched or about which you know a great deal, in which you display your knowledge and understanding.

In your other subjects, you will also be asked to write discursive and factual essays. For example, in History you might be asked to discuss the impact of a particular event, or in Science you may be asked to write a description of a process, such as photosynthesis or the human digestive system, and you will have to write reports of experiments.

In certain subjects, such as Geography, you will have to write analytical essays. You will have to research a particular topic, analyse and evaluate the data you collect and draw conclusions.

Whatever type of essay you have to write, it is important to develop a systematic approach to your writing.

A step-by-step approach to essay-writing

All essay-writing involves a number of stages:

Stage 1 – Identify the type of essay.

- Is it autobiographical? discursive? factual? analytical?
- Think about how you are going to tackle it.

Stage 2 – Collect ideas and information.

- Check through any notes you already have on the topic.
- Do any necessary further research.
- Do a brainstorm.

Stage 3 – Make an outline plan.

- List the main points you are going to make, including the conclusion.
- Work out a logical sequence for presenting the ideas and information.
- Think of a suitable introduction.

Stage 4 – Write the essay.

- Think about the style that is appropriate e.g. the style of an autobiographical essay can be more informal than the style of an analytical essay.

- If it is a coursework essay, do a first draft, then look critically at the content, structure and organisation, before redrafting it. For example, think about changing the order of the ideas, introducing new points, developing and rephrasing ideas.

- If it is an examination essay, be prepared to amend your outline plan if you think of important ideas as you write.

Stage 5 – Edit and proofread.

- Check for grammatical mistakes.
- Check for punctuation errors.
- Check for spelling mistakes

PLANNING A DISCURSIVE ESSAY

IN PAIRS

Practise your essay-planning skills. Study these notes which Dominic made on the subject of euthanasia and make an outline plan for an essay in answer to the question: Should we have the right to choose to end our lives if we are incurably ill or in great pain? Discuss the arguments for and against voluntary euthanasia.

Euthanasia
Definition - the act of killing someone painlessly, especially to relieve suffering from an incurable illness

Religious views
- God created life. Only God can take life. Any deliberate ending of a life is a sin.
- Human life is sacred.
EXIT (Voluntary Euthanasia Society)
Campaigns for euthanasia to be made legal
"An adult person suffering from a severe illness, for which no relief is known, should be entitled by law to the mercy of a painless death, if and only if, that is their expressed wish."
Under present laws anyone who helps a person suffering from a terminal disease to end their life risks prosecution for murder or manslaughter.
House of Lords has rejected bills to legalise euthanasia 3 times.
Advance Directives (living wills)
People can sign advance directives - written requests saying they don't want to be kept alive by artificial means, and that distressing conditions should be controlled by sedation, even if this shortens their lives.
Euthanasia in other countries
- Illegal everywhere except in Northern Territory in Australia.
- Sanctioned in Oregon (USA) and Holland where doctors aren't prosecuted for mercy-killings, but must report them to the police.
Arguments against euthanasia
- Modern painkilling drugs make it possible to relieve suffering and enable people to die with dignity.
- It could put unfair pressure on old people, who become dependent on others, to request it even if they don't really want it.
- It would devalue life. It could be the first step in legalising the elimination of unwanted social groups.
- How could you safeguard against mistakes and abuse? Having two doctors' opinions wouldn't prevent mistakes. It would put doctors in an impossible position.
Arguments in favour of euthanasia
- It can bring a swift and humane end to suffering.
- It can lessen the distress and grief of loved ones who, at present, cannot do anything to help reduce a person's suffering.
- It would enable people who want to do so to die with dignity.

THREE WAYS TO IMPROVE YOUR ESSAY-WRITING

1 Develop an appropriate style

When you are writing essays for GCSE and Standard Grade, it is important to write clearly and concisely. This will help the reader to understand what you are saying, and enable you to write the maximum amount of information in the space and time available.

Follow these guidelines to help keep your writing clear and concise:

- Avoid pompous, wordy statements.
  e.g. After a great deal of thought, I have finally come to the conclusion that there are no grounds for holding such an opinion.

- Avoid repeating words and ideas.

- Do not use slang. The tone of an essay should be formal. Since slang is essentially informal and colloquial, it is out of place and inappropriate in an essay.

- Avoid using abbreviations. In particular, do not use etc. because it suggests that you are not absolutely sure of your facts and have run out of things to say.

- Avoid clichés. A cliché is a phrase that has been used so frequently that it has lost most of its impact. e.g. This was the final straw, the last nail in the coffin.

- Keep quotations short. There is no point in filling your essay up with lengthy quotations. The person marking the essay will know the quotations anyway and is more interested in seeing how you use the quotations to support your arguments than in your showing how good a memory you have got.

- Avoid jargon. Only use technical terms where necessary, otherwise express your ideas in your own words.

2 Work at your punctuation and spelling

Using full stops and commas correctly is essential. It is also important to make sure that your spelling is correct, so that your points can be clearly understood.

- Make sure you always use a full stop at the end of each sentence to separate each complete thought from another.

- Use exclamation marks rarely. They are usually not appropriate in examination essays.

- Commas are used inside sentences for a variety of different purposes. For advice on how to use commas, see *Studywise 1* page 33.

- Semi-colons can be useful, provided that you understand how to use them properly. They can be used to join together two separate ideas, which are closely related, inside a single sentence. e.g. Scientific reports suggest that air pollution is not a major cause of asthma; the main cause of asthma is some kind of allergic reaction.

- Avoid using dashes, either use a comma or start a new sentence.

- While brackets can be used for asides, it is usually better to avoid them and to use commas instead.

- Always use a dictionary to check any words you are not sure how to spell. Work at learning words you misspell by using the LOOK-SAY-COVER-WRITE-SPELL approach, which is explained in *Studywise 1* page 34.

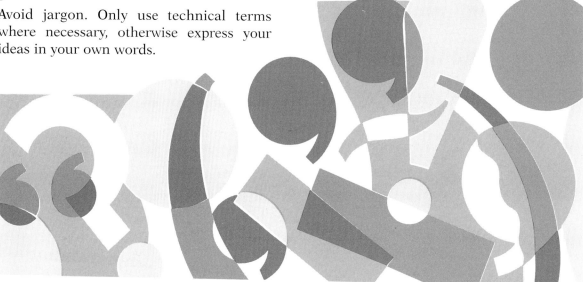

3 Always use standard English grammar

Poor grammar is likely to lose you marks, so always read through essays carefully to check that you have used standard English.

- Avoid dialect expressions which differ from standard English expressions. e.g. Make sure you always use the standard English form of the verb 'to be', avoiding errors such as 'we was' or 'they was'.

- Do not use double negatives.

- Make sure you use the correct past tense for verbs, adding -ed where necessary.

- Avoid split infinitives. i.e. Do not put an adverb between <u>to</u> and a verb as in 'to boldly go'.

- If you have difficulty with grammar, get yourself a simple guide which you can refer to whenever you are unsure about what is correct. A useful book is:

Collins Gem English Grammar by Ronald G Hardie.

An Essay-Writing Checklist

Use this checklist to assess critically the essays you write during your courses. It can be used either at the redrafting stage, if you are writing a coursework essay, or after the essay has been written and marked, if you have been writing a timed examination essay.

Content
- Have you answered the question?
- Is everything you have included relevant?
- Have you missed out anything important?
- Are the facts correct and the quotations accurate?
- Have you supported your ideas with appropriate evidence and examples?

Structure and Organisation
- Does the introduction give a clear indication of what is to follow?
- Are the points presented in a logical order?
- Is each major point developed in a separate paragraph?
- Is the essay well balanced so that different points of view are considered?
- Does the conclusion provide an effective summary of your answer to the question?

Style and presentation
- Are the language and style appropriate to the type of essay?
- Are any quotations presented properly with their sources correctly acknowledged?
- Have you avoided using clichés, jargon and slang?
- Are the grammar, punctuation and spelling correct?

•• IN PAIRS ••

Each choose an examination essay that has been marked and returned to you. Using the checklist, identify the strengths and weaknesses of the essay and then show your essay to your partner and discuss your assessment of it with them.

WRITING ESSAYS IN EXAMINATIONS

Examiners report that the main reason why candidates lose marks in essay questions is because they do not answer the question. When you read an essay question, it is important to pick out the key words which indicate the approach the examiner wants you to take and how they expect you to answer the question.

IN PAIRS

Study the list of key terms that examiners use in essay questions. Choose a subject which you are both studying and look at the essay questions on either a past paper or a specimen paper. Talk about the way the questions are phrased and the type of answers that are expected.

Account for

Justify

Trace

Key terms used in examination questions:

Account for: give the reasons why.

Analyse : break down into parts, investigate in order to discover the essential features.

Assess: weigh up the evidence and give your opinion about the merit of different theories and views.

Compare: look at the similarities (and, therefore, also the differences) between things.

Contrast: show the differences between.

Criticise: consider all the evidence and the different opinions and give your own opinion.

Define: state exactly the meaning of something.

Describe: give a detailed account of, for example, events or a process.

Discuss: define the issues, look at the arguments on both sides, examine the implications, and try to reach a conclusion.

Evaluate: weigh up the arguments and give your opinions about how good each argument is.

Examine: look closely at the issues and draw a conclusion.

Explain: give the reasons for.

Illustrate: explain and give examples.

Justify: show the reasons for a particular point of view, at the same time arguing against the opposite point of view.

Outline: explain the main features, without going into too much detail.

Relate: i) tell or narrate ii) show the connections between two things.

Summarise: list the key points, without going into detail.

Trace: give an account of the history or development of something.

WRITING TECHNICAL REPORTS

In some subjects, such as technology, you will be expected to produce a written report of a practical assignment or project which you have carried out. Your report should give clear, simple explanations of everything you planned to do and everything you actually did.

In many cases, your teacher will explain the format that you should use for your report. However, if you are not told how to present your report, you can use the following customary format for any technical or scientific report.

A format for a technical or scientific report

Title page: On the first page give a heading that shows clearly the subject of the report: 'Report on the production of...', 'Report of an investigation into...'.

Contents page: List the contents of the report, giving relevant page or paragraph numbers. Complete this page last.

Your brief: Describe what you were attempting to do.

Your analysis: Analyse the problem you faced and include the research material you have gathered.

Your thinking: Discuss your initial thinking, explaining your ideas for possible solutions and your evaluation of them.

Your solution: Explain how you developed your solution.

Your evidence: Include drawings and any other evidence of your solution e.g. photographs. This section is particularly important when you have produced something, such as a model, which cannot be sent to the external marker.

Your evaluation: Give an objective evaluation of your solution.

Before you submit your report, reread it to ensure that it develops logically. Also, correct any obvious errors or omissions. Look at the syllabus to confirm that you have complied with all the instructions and that you have demonstrated the required skills and abilities. Remember that examiners are told to reward candidates for their successes, not penalise them for their failures: so be positive and make sure that your report shows what you can do.

●● IN PAIRS ●●

In which of your subjects do you have to write a report of a practical assignment or project? Choose one of them and look at the syllabus together. Discuss what you are required to do and what particular skills and abilities you are expected to demonstrate.

6 Developing your oral skills

TALKS AND PRESENTATIONS

● ON YOUR OWN ●

Plan and draft a 5 minute talk to give to your class on either a topic of your own choice or on one of the topics listed below. Decide whether you want your talk to be primarily informative, entertaining or persuasive. Write it out in full, then write the main points on separate cards and practise giving your talk to someone e.g. a parent or friend, using notes rather than the complete script.

Topics

Stereotyping	Prejudice
Friendship	Women's rights
Leisure	Pollution
Keeping fit	Crime
Parents	Gambling
The future	Homelessness

As part of your GCSE or Standard Grade English course you may be required to give a prepared talk. You will either be given a topic or allowed to choose your own topic. You may also be asked to give oral presentations in other subjects, for example to give a report of what you found out from a survey in your Geography fieldwork. These two pages focus on the skills of preparing and delivering a talk.

PLANNING YOUR TALK

In many ways, planning and preparing a talk is like planning and preparing an essay. The content and structure of your talk will depend on three things: the topic, the purpose of the talk and the audience you are addressing.

Once you have decided on a topic, the next thing you must think about is your purpose. Do you want your talk to be informative, entertaining or persuasive? Is the aim to describe some personal experiences or to convey information which you have researched? Do you want to simply convey facts or to put across a point of view in order to try to convince the audience to support your argument? The way you structure your talk and the language you use will depend on what your purpose is.

Similarly, you need to think about your audience and the context in which you are giving your talk. You will vary your approach if your talk is to be given to an audience of parents in the school hall one evening rather than to your classmates in a lesson.

DRAFTING YOUR TALK

Drafting your talk is like drafting an essay. It needs to have a clear structure:

● an <u>introduction</u> which will grab the audience's attention;

● a <u>main body</u> which conveys the information, describes the experiences or expresses the argument or point of view;

● a <u>conclusion</u> which not only rounds off the talk, but creates an impact on the audience.

Many people find it useful to draft a talk by writing it out in full. But remember you are giving a talk, not reading out an essay, so once you have worked out the structure of your talk it's a good idea to split it up into sections and to note down on pieces of card the two or three main points you are going to make in each section. You'll find it easier to keep eye-contact with the audience and to engage their attention if you use cards with notes on them rather than pieces of A4 paper with the complete talk on them.

As you are drafting your talk, think about whether you could use any visual aids to help you to convey your ideas or information. Make sure that the writing on any posters you prepare is not only legible but large enough for people at the back of the audience to read. Consider using an overhead projector rather than a poster or chart. It is often easier for an audience to read something put up on a screen rather than pinned to a board.

DELIVERING YOUR TALK

The effectiveness of your talk will depend not only on its content and structure, but on how you deliver it. You need to think about how you can use your voice and your body language to gain and maintain the audience's attention. Things you need to think about are:

- Clarity
- Volume
- Pace
- Tone
- Emphasis
- Eye-contact
- Gestures
- Posture

●● IN PAIRS ●●

Draw up a list of Dos and Don'ts when delivering a talk. Then, share your ideas in a class discussion and agree a class list of 'Dos and Don'ts when giving a talk'.

Evaluating your performance

Whenever someone has to give a talk, you can use this checklist to evaluate their performance. Start by commenting on two or three things that you feel the speaker did well, then identify one or two things that you think the speaker needs to improve. Offer practical suggestions saying what the speaker needs to do in order to improve their performance.

❨TALK EVALUATION❩
✔Checklist

Content and structure
1. Was the speaker's purpose clear? Did the speaker achieve their aim?
2. How well did the speaker know the topic? Had they done enough preparation and research?
3. Did the introduction immediately capture your attention?
4. Were the points in the main body of the talk presented in a logical order?
5. Were the ideas and information in the talk easy to understand? Was each point explained clearly?
6. Did the speaker make good use of examples or evidence to explain or illustrate their points?
7. Was the conclusion of the talk effective? Did it have a strong impact on the audience?
8. Were the language and tone of the talk appropriate to the audience and context?

Delivery
1. Did the speaker speak clearly and loudly enough?
2. Did they speak with plenty of expression? Was there enough variety in the tone and pitch of their voice?
3. Was the talk delivered at the right pace? Did the speaker talk too fast or too slowly?
4. Did the speaker maintain eye-contact with the audience?
5. Did the speaker adopt and maintain a confident and relaxed posture?
6. Did the speaker make effective use of techniques, such as pauses, gestures or deliberate raising of their voice to emphasise particular points?
7. Did the speaker make good use of any visual aids they had prepared? Would the talk have been more effective if they had made use of visual aids?

DEBATING

During your GCSE or Standard Grade courses, you are likely to have to prepare a speech expressing a point of view or to take part in a debate. These two pages focus on the skills of preparing a speech for a debate.

Claptraps

A writer called Max Atkinson spent some time analysing the speeches of politicians to see what went down well with audiences. He watched hundreds of video tapes of political speeches and looked into what it is that makes an audience clap. He came up with some theories about 'claptrap', the way in which speakers can 'trap' their audiences into clapping or responding to a speech.

Claptrap techniques:

1 Listing things in threes, e.g. 'Labour will spend and spend, and borrow and borrow, and tax and tax.' (Norman Tebbit, Conservative politician, UK General Election 1983).

2 Saying things in contrastive pairs, e.g. 'That's one small step for man. One giant leap for mankind.' (Neil Armstrong, US astronaut, Moon broadcast 1969)

3 Talking positively about 'us' to make the audience identify with what is being said, e.g. 'We shall pay any price, bear any burden, meet any hardship, support any friend, oppose any foe, to assure the survival and success of liberty.' (John F Kennedy, inaugural address as US President, 1961)

4 Talking negatively about 'them', e.g. '...there are two Conservative parties in this election. One is offering the continuation of policies we've had for the last five years, and the other is offering a return to policies of forty years ago.' (David Steel, Liberal politician, UK General Election, 1979)

Atkinson also found that newspapers and TV news took their quotes mainly from the lists of three and contrastive pairs that appeared in speeches.

IN PAIRS

Read and discuss the information about claptraps. Then read Sam Yorke's speech 'Why I am against capital punishment'. Pick out the points in her speech where she uses the techniques which Atkinson identified as claptraps.

Discuss how she begins and ends her speech. Which do you find more effective – her beginning or her ending?

Imagine you are news reporters. Which parts of her speech would make good quotes to use as 'soundbites' in a news report of her speech?

Why I'm against capital punishment

'There's no crime worse than murder. But there's no punishment worse than the death penalty. If we execute murderers, then aren't we ourselves acting like murderers? The law condemns murder, then goes on to murder in the name of the law.

Most people who want to see the death penalty reintroduced do so because they want revenge. They argue that the law should be based on the principle of 'an eye for an eye, a tooth for a tooth'. But surely there is more to it than that. The aim of punishment should be to protect society, to deter potential murderers and to reform criminals, not to exact revenge. That's why I believe that murderers should get life imprisonment, and by life imprisonment, I mean a life sentence, not one that allows them to be released after a certain number of years.

Another important reason why it would be wrong to bring back the death penalty is because mistakes can be made and innocent people can be executed. Some people say that anyone convicted of terrorist atrocities should be hanged. But look at what would have happened in the cases of the Birmingham six and the Guildford four. The wrong people would have been executed.

It is sometimes argued that the death penalty acts as a deterrent. But there is no evidence that the number of murders is significantly higher than it was before the death penalty was abolished - apart from terrorist offences. But I don't think it is a good idea to execute terrorists convicted of murder. It would only make them into martyrs.

Capital punishment has no place in a civilised society. It is cruel, barbaric and inhumane. There is no humane way of executing someone. Sometimes the electric chair or hanging does not work and it causes the prisoner great pain and increases their family's distress.

All killing is wrong and capital punishment is a form of killing. We should not bring it back.'

Sam Yorke

ON YOUR OWN

Prepare a speech for a debate on one of the topics listed below. Start by researching the topic thoroughly in order to discover the facts about it. Be on the look-out for arguments and pieces of evidence you can use to support your point of view. Think about the arguments people might try to use against your point of view and note down anything you can use to counter these arguments. Then draft your speech, trying to use some of the techniques you have learned from studying the information about claptraps.

Topics for debate

- The National Lottery should be abolished.
- Boxing should be banned.
- Voluntary euthanasia should be made legal.
- Proportional representation should be introduced for parliamentary elections.

7 Revising

Work with someone who is studying a subject that you are not studying. Take it in turns to tell each other about the syllabus in that subject and about the types of questions you will have to do in the exam.

The key to successful revision is organisation and planning. In order to plan your revision and use your time effectively, you need to know exactly what you will have to do in all your examinations.

FINDING OUT ABOUT EXAMS

There are two ways of finding out about an exam: by studying the syllabus and by looking at past exam papers.

1 The syllabus

The syllabus is a booklet from the examination board which tells you the topics you must study, the form the examination will take and the percentage of marks that will be given for each part of the exam. Make sure you understand what the syllabus is for each of the subjects you are studying. If you are not clear exactly what you need to do in a particular subject, ask your teacher if you can look at a copy of the syllabus. When you are studying the syllabus, note down details of anything you do not understand and of any topics you do not think you have covered and ask your teacher about them.

2 Past papers

Get hold of a number of past papers for each subject (or of specimen papers if the syllabus is a new one) and analyse them to see what type of questions you will have to answer and which topics come up regularly. The type of questions you have to answer will vary from subject to subject. Some questions will involve recalling information e.g. in Science you might be asked to explain how the human digestive system works. Other questions will ask you to apply skills that you have learned e.g. you may be presented with geographical or historical information and asked to use your skills to interpret it. In some subjects you may be set multiple-choice questions which ask you to recognise the correct answer from a number of alternatives. Once you know what types of questions you are going to be asked in a particular subject, you can build in time during your revision programme for that subject to practise answering those types of questions.

Making a revision calendar

In the period immediately before the examinations, you need to plan your revision very carefully in order to ensure that you will have enough time to cover all your subjects. So it's a good idea to draw up a revision calendar for the 10-12 weeks prior to the examinations. This period will include the Easter holidays. You should allow yourself some time for relaxation in the holidays, but a large amount of your time should be set aside for revision.

1 See if you can obtain a large calendar or year planner that you can pin on the wall next to where you study.

2 Mark in the dates and times of your exams.

3 Shade in dates and times when you know you have other commitments e.g family outings, sports events, club meetings.

4 Make a list of all the topics in each subject which you need to revise and of approximately how much time you think you need to spend on each topic. Plan to spend more time on your weaker subjects than on your stronger ones.

5 Calculate how many hours you have available and how much time you are going to allocate to each subject.

6 Decide on the order in which you are going to tackle your subjects and the topics within them. Then, using a pencil, begin to draft your revision timetable by writing on the calendar which subjects and topics you plan to revise each day. To keep up your interest it is better to plan to revise a variety of different topics each day rather than to spend a whole day on just one topic.

7 Try to leave one or two revision slots for each week blank, so that you can use them either for extra revision of a difficult topic or for revision of a topic that you missed revising earlier in the week, because you were unable to stick to your timetable for some reason.

8 Be sure to leave yourself some time for rest and leisure, particularly in the last few days before the exams.

IN PAIRS

Each draft a revision calendar for the weeks immediately before the exams. Then, discuss your revision plans together and suggest any alterations that you think might improve them.

Working in revision groups

A useful way of revising is to plan revision sessions with one or two other people who are doing the same course as you. Working alongside someone else can be very useful. But if you arrange to do so, you need to be very disciplined to make sure that you actually spend the time working rather than chatting or listening to CDs.

It is important to decide before each session what topic you are going to focus on. Otherwise, you can waste a lot of time. If you know what you're going to be doing, there are a number of useful ways you can prepare for the session. For example, you could each prepare revision cards or answers to a particular exam question and then use part of the session to compare them. Alternatively, you could each prepare a quick quiz to test the knowledge of the others on a topic. While you are looking through your notes in order to

work out the questions for the quiz, you'll be doing some useful revision.

Another useful way of spending a session is to take it in turns to teach each other a particular topic. Having to work out how to explain the topic will help you to understand it as well as to learn it.

It can also be valuable psychologically to work as a member of a revision group in at least one of your subjects, rather than to spend all your time revising on your own. Talking to other people can help to lessen the anxiety that can build up if you are isolated while revising.

IN PAIRS

Discuss the idea of working in a revision group. What do you see as the advantages and disadvantages? For which of the subjects you are studying do you think it would be the most useful to form a revision group?

AN ACTIVE APPROACH TO REVISION

Before you start a revision session it is important to decide not only what you are going to revise, but how you are going to revise it. Your approach will depend on the subject you are studying and the type of questions you are going to be asked in the exam. For example, if you are studying a biological topic you might decide to focus on learning about a particular system, then testing yourself by drawing a diagram or flowchart. If you are revising maths, then your focus will probably be on practising how to solve a particular type of problem.

Always give your revision session a focus. Don't just sit down and start revising by reading and re-reading your notes over and over again in the hope that you'll gradually learn them. Not only is this boring, it's not a good way of learning, because you are not actively involved in using the information and ideas that you are trying to learn.

A step-by-step revision strategy

Use these steps to develop an active approach to your revision.

Step 1 – Find a focus
Decide on a focus for your revision. Look at past papers and write down the specific questions you want to be able to answer when you have done your revision. Think about what you are going to do during the revision session in order to check that you have understood and can remember what you have been learning.

Step 2 – Study your notes
Read carefully through your notes. Use a pencil or highlighter to underline or highlight key facts and important terms.

Step 3 – Make revision cards
Go through your notes again, picking out the essential points, and make a revision card containing the key ideas and information you need to learn. Condensing your notes will help you to think about and to understand what you are trying to learn and to begin to commit it to memory.

Card no 17

16 April 1996

Manufacture of sulphuric acid (H_2SO_4)

① Burn sulphur in air → sulphur dioxide

$$S + O_2 \rightarrow SO_2$$

② Heat SO_2 in air + catalyst → sulphur trioxide
(to 450°C) (Vanadium Oxide)

$$2SO_2 + O_2 \rightarrow 2SO_3$$

③ SO_3 reacts with water → sulphuric acid

$$SO_3 + H_2O \rightarrow H_2SO_4$$

N.B. Stage 3 almost explosive ∴ done in 2 stages using sulphuric acid (small amount) as catalyst:

i) $SO_3 + H_2SO_4 \rightarrow H_2S_2O_7$
(disulphuric acid)

ii) $H_2S_2O_7 + H_2O \rightarrow 2H_2SO_4$

H_2SO_4 used in manufacture of other chemicals e.g. fertilizers, plastics

Step 4 – Learn it!

Study your revision cards in order to learn them. Use any methods of remembering things that work for you, such as making up your own mnemonics. A mnemonic is a word or phrase made from a set of letters based on a list. e.g. <u>E</u>very <u>G</u>ood <u>B</u>oy <u>D</u>eserves <u>F</u>avour is a mnemonic which is used to help beginners learn the five lines of the treble stave in music - EGBDF.

Often you'll be trying to remember a particular number of points – for example, the different stages of a process in Science or a list of the causes of an event in History. Identifying how many points are involved can be useful when you are trying to remember them.

Step 5 – Test yourself

Put away the revision cards and test yourself. A very good way of testing your knowledge and understanding is to practise using what you have learned by doing a practice question from a past paper. Alternatively, you can try to write out the key points from memory or to draw a diagram or chart, or you can ask a friend or relative to test you. Exactly how you test yourself will depend on the subject and topic, and the type of questions that you will be asked on that topic.

Step 6 – Check it!

Whatever method of testing you've been using, you need to look again at your revision cards to check that you got the facts right and that you didn't miss out anything important. Use a pencil or higlighter to mark any important points which you did not remember or got wrong. Then, if necessary, repeat steps 4, 5 and 6 until you are sure you have learned what you need to know.

Dear Gita

I always spend a lot of time revising whenever we come to the end of a topic, but I never seem to get good marks in tests and I'm worried I'm going to do badly in the exams. I spend hours copying out my essays and trying to learn them and I read through my notes over and over again, but I just don't seem to be able to take it all in. It's really getting me down. Although I usually work non-stop for several hours each evening before the test, it doesn't seem to make any difference. I feel like giving up. Please can you help me.

Andrea

● ●   IN PAIRS   ● ●

Work with someone who is doing the same course as you. Choose a topic and each study your notes on that topic and produce a set of revision cards. Then, compare your revision cards and take it in turns to use the revision cards to test each other on the topic.

● ●   IN PAIRS   ● ●

Discuss Andrea's problem and draft a reply to it, then share your replies in a whole class discussion.

● ● ●   IN GROUPS   ● ● ●

What problems do members of the group have with revision? Make a list of problems and discuss ways of dealing with them.

Draw up a list of Dos and Don'ts – How to tackle revision.

8 Coping with exam pressures

MANAGING STRESS

As the exams approach it is natural for you to feel some anxiety and apprehension. A certain amount of anxiety is useful. It helps to keep you on your toes and can improve your performance. If you didn't feel at all concerned about getting good grades, then you probably wouldn't work as hard as you need to work in order to get them.

But anxiety can get out of hand. The pressures of meeting coursework deadlines and keeping to a revision schedule can cause some people to start worrying too much. When this happens, they can start suffering from stress, which can seriously affect their performance.

Many students who start getting in a state about exams make matters worse because of irrational beliefs. Irrational beliefs about exams can convince people who are feeling very anxious that there is nothing they can do to stop themselves doing badly. In reality, their anxiety is based on myths and there is plenty they can do to help themselves.

Some common myths about exams

'Exams are a random process – you could get asked a question about anything at all, even stuff that you've never heard of.'

Not true. All GCSE exams follow a set syllabus, and examiners are not allowed to go beyond it in asking questions. Make sure that you get yourself a copy of the syllabus that you are supposed to be following in each subject, and use it to check that you've revised everything you will need. If your exam contains questions which go beyond the syllabus, you can complain to the Exam Board.

'Exams are just luck anyway.'

No they aren't. If you have followed your course and understood it, and if you have revised properly, trained yourself in exam skills and managed your anxiety effectively, you can guarantee that you will pass. Most people take chances that they don't need to take; maybe they only revise a restricted number of topics and gamble on the right questions coming up, or they leave all their revision to the last minute and hope for the best. Obviously, if you do that then things will be risky. But it's your choice – you can make certain you will pass if you go about things in the right way.

'The mark you get will depend on whether the examiner is in a good mood or not.'

Not true. GCSE examiners are carefully checked, and are given the sack if they aren't marking consistently. Examiners apply the same standards to every paper that they mark. They always use a marking scheme which lays down very carefully what will gain credit. The mark you get will depend on what you have written and whether it answers the questions properly or not – nothing else.

> **'** *I always get in a state about exams. There's nothing I can do about it – I'm just like that.* **'**
>
> On the contrary there's a lot you can do about it. You can change how you tackle exams. You can adopt anxiety-relieving strategies, you can build up your confidence, and you can make sure that things don't end up going completely wrong at the last minute by planning ahead.

> **'** *Some people just have naturally good memories, and I'm not one of them.* **'**
>
> Highly unlikely. Your memory for your social life and the things that matter to you is probably just fine. What you actually mean is that you don't find it easy to remember stuff that seems irrelevant and meaningless to you. Nor do I, and nor does anyone else. But if you understand what you're doing and why it matters, and use proper revision techniques, you'll find your memory is as good as anyone else's.

How does stress affect you?

If a person is suffering from stress, it will start to affect the way they behave. However, different people react to stress in different ways. Some people become angry and irritable, while others become depressed and withdrawn.

Being stressed can affect how you feel about yourself. People under stress often lose confidence in their ability to do things and become very negative about their chances of success, so they find it harder to motivate themselves.

Their work can suffer in a number of ways. They may find themselves worrying so much that they keep on putting off getting down to work or find it hard to concentrate when they eventually do. They may spend their time unproductively – for example, meticulously reading and making notes on whole chapters, instead of systematically searching for and identifying key points. Frequently, they will end a study session feeling dissatisfied with what they've done, instead of recognising what they have achieved.

Stress can affect you physically too. You may get headaches or indigestion or may feel exhausted from lack of sleep, because you lie awake at night worrying. Feeling tense puts a strain on your whole system so you are more likely to pick up colds and other viral infections.

The important thing to do if you are suffering from stress is to recognise that you are and to take steps to deal with it (see pages 42-3).

(see pages 42-3).

●●● IN GROUPS ●●●

Read and talk about each of the myths about exams. Then discuss each of these statements in turn and say why you agree or disagree with it:

1   You'll only do well in a subject if you like the teacher.

2   Success in exams depends on good study habits.

3   If you are struggling in a subject, there's no point in trying.

4   You'll only succeed if you get lots of help from your parents.

5   Success in exams is a matter of luck.

6   Failure is usually caused by bad teaching.

7   Success stems from determination and self-discipline.

8   People who fail often blame the exam, but it's usually their own fault.

9   You'll only succeed in exams if you are prepared to give up everything to do so.

SIX WAYS OF HANDLING STRESS

Coping with stress involves identifying what is causing the stress, taking action to prevent it occurring and developing techniques to manage your stress.

1 Get Organised

The major cause of stress among GCSE and Standard Grade students is the feeling that there isn't enough time to do the necessary work.

- Identify very busy periods when your workload is going to be particularly heavy and see if you can renegotiate any of your deadlines. You may, for example, be able to postpone handing in a practice essay in one subject to enable you to cope with the pressure of finishing a piece of coursework in another subject.
- Draw up an action plan to improve your time-management (see Units 1 and 7). Plan ahead and set yourself goals to be achieved by specific dates.

2 Think positively

The more confident you feel, the less likely you are to feel stressed and the more likely you are to succeed.

- Recognise what you have achieved so far. Make a list of tasks and tick them off as you finish them.
  Give yourself something to look forward to. For example, when you complete a long assignment, give yourself a treat, such as a trip to the cinema.

- Take action to relieve your stress. For instance, if you have got a problem in a particular subject plan how to deal with it and do something about it, instead of just letting it prey on your mind.

- Keep your problems in perspective. When you have problems in one or two areas, remind yourself of some of your other subjects in which things are going well.

3 Keep fit and healthy

- Take regular exercise. When you are under stress, your body produces a number of different hormones, including adrenaline. Regular exercise, such as swimming or dancing, is the best way of getting rid of the biochemical effects of stress, so that you won't feel so tense.

- Eat a balanced diet. Hunger increases stress, so it's very important to eat regular meals and to make sure you have a balanced diet. If you're hungry and stressed, you're less likely to be able to concentrate properly. Also, when you are stressed, your body uses up lots of blood sugar because you are burning up energy faster than usual, so you shouldn't worry if you eat rather more than usual.

- Get plenty of sleep. If you start staying up late on a regular basis in order to get your work done, then it's bound to affect your performance. If you're too tired, you won't be able to study effectively. Remember, too, to give yourself time to

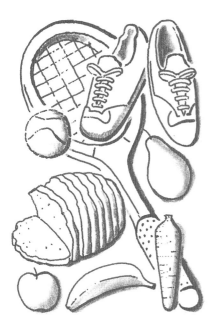

unwind before trying to go to sleep, instead of working right up to the last minute before you switch the light off.

4 Learn to relax

● Allow yourself time for relaxation. If you spend all your time working or worrying about your work, then you will become increasingly stressed. You need to find the right balance between time spent working and time spent on your leisure.

● Learn relaxation techniques. If you are getting so stressed that you find it hard to relax even at the times you have set aside for your leisure, then it is worth learning some relaxation techniques. You can find advice on how to relax in books for teenagers, such as *Dare to be You, a handbook for teenage health*, by Susannah Kenton (Hodder).

5 Stay in control

● Take responsibility for dealing with your stress. It's no good blaming external circumstances for causing your stress. You need to take the responsibility to do something about them. Have realistic expectations and set reachable targets. Don't try to change everything at once. Identify what is causing your stress and take steps to change things gradually.

● Be assertive. If your stress is caused by parental pressure, avoid getting into unproductive arguments. Try to keep calm, listen to what your parents have to say, try to understand their point of view, and then put forward your point of view assertively rather than aggressively.

6 Talk it over

● Find someone to talk to. It's often said that a problem shared is a problem halved. Find an adult – a parent, a family friend, a teacher or your doctor – who you feel would listen to you sympathetically, and tell them why you are feeling anxious and stressed.

● Ask for advice. Ask their advice and discuss ways of dealing with your stress. Then, make up your own mind what you are going to do about it.

> *Note: In extreme cases of stress, it is worth having some counselling in order to help you to cope with your problems. For advice on counselling services in your area, write to The National Association of Young People's Counselling and Advisory Services (NAYPCAS), 17-23 Albion Street, Leicester LE1 6GD.*

○○ IN PAIRS ○○

Read and discuss the advice given on these pages on how to handle stress. Then role play a scene in which a student who is feeling very stressed because of work pressures talks to an adult and asks them for advice.

Dealing with pressure from parents

Tensions can build up at home, because your parents are anxious about whether or not you are doing enough studying to succeed.

'My parents keep telling me to turn my music off. They think I can't work with it on. We keep having rows about it.'

'They won't let me have some of my friends round any more, because they think they're a bad influence and they stop me working.'

'They expect me to stay in my bedroom all night every night.'

'They keep on and on about how well my sister did and how I don't study as much as she did.'

'They're always nagging and trying to run my life for me.'

○○○ IN GROUPS ○○○

Discuss these statements and talk about any ways in which your parents put pressure on you when you are working at home. Suggest ways of dealing with problems caused by parental pressure.

9 Examinations

LEARNING FROM THE TRIAL EXAMS

The trial exams (mocks) will help you to identify those subjects in which you are doing well and those subjects which you need to concentrate on improving. They also help you to develop the techniques you need when tackling exams. Many students who do poorly in the trial exams still go on to get good grades in the exams themselves. So it is worth reviewing your results in order to identify what you can do to make sure you get the grades you are capable of getting in the actual exam.

REVIEWING YOUR RESULTS

Use this checklist of questions to help you to review your results and to identify the reasons why you didn't do as well as you had hoped in one of your subjects:

- Did you follow the instructions properly?
- Did you complete all the questions?
- Did you make the right choice of questions?
- Did you misunderstand some of the questions?
- Were some of your answers badly planned and illogical, because you rushed into writing them, instead of spending time thinking and planning?
- Did you answer some questions in too much detail and others in not enough detail?
- Did you miss out important points in some of your answers?
- Did you run out of time because you didn't plan carefully enough?
- Did you make careless mistakes because you didn't check your answers?
- Did your memory let you down because you hadn't done enough revision?
- Did you panic and start making silly mistakes?

Learning from your teacher's feedback

When you get your papers back, make the most of the opportunity to learn from the feedback you get from your teacher.

- Read and learn from the comments your teacher has written on your paper.
- Listen carefully to the points your teacher makes as they go over the paper in class.

ON YOUR OWN

Choose one of your subjects in which you were disappointed with your results. Go through the paper(s) using the checklist to help you to analyse why you didn't do as well as you could have done. Then, write a short statement saying how you plan to tackle the paper(s) differently in the actual exam. List at least three things you are going to do to help to improve your performance. Then, discuss your plans with a partner.

- Make notes in the margin of points you missed out. (Note where you could have picked up more marks on your good answers as well as on your poor answers.)

- Note the points your teacher makes on the questions you did not choose as well as on the ones you did choose.

- Use some of your study time to go through the papers, analysing why you did well or did badly. A good way of doing this is to work with a friend, learning from each other's good answers as well as from your mistakes.

- If you are still puzzled about why you didn't do well, make an appointment to see your teacher and go through the paper with them.

Preparing for the examinations

As part of your final preparation for the exams, you need to make sure you are absolutely clear what each exam paper requires you to do. You will already have studied past papers in order to focus your revision on the types of question they ask. Nevertheless, it is worth spending time taking another look in order to remind yourself exactly how the paper is set out and of any detailed instructions which you have to follow.

Ten things you need to know about each exam paper:

1 How long does the paper last?

2 Is the paper divided into separate parts?

3 Do you have to answer questions from every section?

4 Are any of the questions compulsory?

5 How many questions do you have to answer?

6 How many marks are there for each question?

7 What types of question are there?

8 What form do your answers to the questions have to take?

9 How long are you advised to spend on each question?

10 What equipment do you need to take in to the exam? (In addition to pens, pencils, ruler etc, are you allowed to take in anything such as an unmarked copy of the set text, a calculator or a dictionary?)

●●	**IN PAIRS**	●●

Choose a subject you are both studying. Go through a past paper or a specimen paper and use the checklist to help you to draw up an exam paper check card similar to the example shown. Then, on your own, study past papers or specimen papers for your other subjects and produce exam paper check cards for each of them.

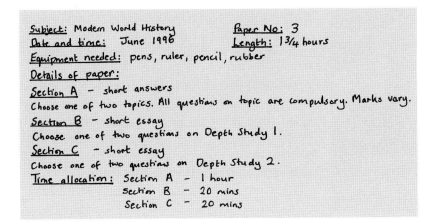

Subject: Modern World History Paper No: 3
Date and time: June 1996 Length: 1¾ hours
Equipment needed: pens, ruler, pencil, rubber
Details of paper:
Section A — short answers
Choose one of two topics. All questions on topic are compulsory. Marks vary.
Section B — short essay
Choose one of two questions on Depth Study 1.
Section C — short essay
Choose one of two questions on Depth Study 2.
Time allocation: Section A — 1 hour
         Section B — 20 mins
         Section C — 20 mins

TAKING EXAMINATIONS

BEFORE THE EXAM

The most important thing is to make sure you don't enter the exam room feeling flustered and anxious. Try to get a good night's sleep, then get up at your usual time, have a proper breakfast and allow yourself plenty of time to get to school. Try to arrive at the exam room a few minutes early, but avoid getting drawn into conversations about revision and the questions you might get. Such conversations tend only to increase anxiety.

When you are allowed into the room, settle yourself at your desk, lay out the equipment you are going to need and set your watch to agree with the exam room clock.

IN THE EXAMINATION

There are a number of examination techniques that you can develop, which can increase the chances of your getting the grades you deserve.

Making a systematic start

Often, students are so anxious to start writing that they don't read the questions properly or they pick questions that aren't the right ones for them. It is important to be systematic and not to rush.

A step-by-step approach:

1. Read the instructions at the front of the paper to remind yourself which sections you must do and how many questions you have to answer. (Don't assume you'll remember what you've got to do. Every year some students fail exams they could have passed simply because they answered too many or too few questions.)

2. Read carefully through all the questions in the sections of the paper that you have to do.

3. If there is a choice of questions, put ticks beside those that are possibles and crosses beside those you definitely do not want to do.

4. Re-read the questions you think you might do. Underline any key words in the question. Notice, also, if there are separate parts to the question. (It is worth spending time doing this, as many students fail exams because they misinterpret the questions and, therefore, do not give the correct answers.)

5. Choose the questions you are going to do and decide the order in which you are going to do them. It's a good idea to start with the questions you feel most confident about, as these are likely to be the ones for which you'll get the most marks.

Sticking to a time plan

To ensure that you answer the required amount of questions, you need to have a time plan. The instructions on the first page of many papers advise you approximately how long you should spend on each question. Either follow these instructions or make your own time plan by dividing your time carefully between the questions you have to answer, bearing in mind the type of questions and the number of marks for each question. Since time is precious in the exam, you should work out your time plan as part of your preparation before the exam. Then, when the exam starts, write it down on a piece of scrap paper, so that you can refer to it during the exam.

The example shows a time plan for a 1 hr 45 mins exam in which candidates are required to answer three questions – a short answers question with two parts a and b (Q.1) worth 40% of the marks and two longer essay-type questions (Q.2, Q.3) each worth 30% of the marks.

Time plan - Paper 1		
9.15 — 9.20	Reading time
9.20 — 9.35	Q.1a
9.35 — 9.50	Q.1b
9.50 — 10.20	Q.2
10.20 — 10.50	Q.3
10.50 — 11.00	Checking time

During the exam, check now and then to see that you are sticking to your time-plan. If you find that you are beginning to run out of time, stop and revise your plan. Bear in mind that you will probably pick up more marks by finishing the paper and answering one or two questions concisely than you would if you left one of the questions unanswered. So if you are running out of time, either write short answers to the remaining questions or answer them in note-form.

Planning your answers

When you are tackling questions that require longer answers, such as essays, it is essential to spend a few minutes planning your answer so it will be coherent and logical.

A step-by-step approach:

1 Look again at the question, focusing on the key words that you underlined, in order to ensure that you understand the type of answer that is required. e.g. Does it require an analytical or factual answer? Does the question provide a structure for your answer?

2 Take a piece of spare paper and do a brainstorm, noting the points you are going to make in your answer in any order, as they come into your mind.

3 Look through your list of points and decide on the best order in which to put them. Don't write the list out again, simply write

numbers beside each point to indicate in which paragraph or section of the answer you should put it. Make sure that the point which you put last is an appropriate conclusion to the answer.

4 Think of a suitable introductory sentence or paragraph and start writing.

Planning your answer will keep you focused on answering the question, help you to think clearly and make you feel more confident and calm. It also helps you to avoid repeating yourself, by making you aware of what you have included in each part of your answer.

Showing your thinking

In some of your exams, particularly those in which you have to do calculations, it is important to show the steps by which you reached the answer. In maths, for example, you can pick up lots of marks by showing that you know how to tackle a problem, even if you make an error at some stage which causes you to get the wrong answer. So, however good you are at working things out in your head, don't just write down the answer, make sure you show how you worked it out.

Similarly, in other exams, always support your statements and give reasons why you hold particular views or have reached a particular conclusion. Include evidence and examples and quote the sources of key ideas and significant pieces of information.

At the end of the exam

Read through what you have written. Check for spelling and punctuation errors, that you have numbered your answers correctly and that you haven't missed out any part of a question.

When you leave the room, don't get drawn into conversations about the exam, as they are only likely to make you feel anxious. Give yourself a break and try to do something relaxing, before getting yourself ready for the next exam.

• • •   **IN GROUPS**   • • •

Read and discuss the advice that is given on these pages. Which do you think are the most helpful pieces of advice?

Either draw up a list of Dos and Don'ts – How to Tackle Exams or a list of your Top Ten Tips for Tackling Exams.

10 Your progress and achievements

REVIEWING YOUR PROGRESS

At certain points during your GCSE or Standard Grade courses, your teachers will write reports on your progress. You and your parents will also have the opportunity to discuss your progress with your teachers at parents' consultation evenings. This can be invaluable as it can help identify your strengths and weaknesses and the areas you need to target for improvement.

The value of such reviews can be increased if you prepare for them by carrying out self-assessments. You can use the self-assessment guidelines (below) either to help you to write your own reports on your progress in your subjects, which you can use as the basis for comparison with your subject teachers' reports, or to draw up a list of points about your progress in a particular subject, which you would like to raise with your subject teacher at a parents' consultation evening.

SELF-ASSESSMENT GUIDELINES

- Look again at the syllabus to remind yourself of the *skills* and the *knowledge and understanding* which you are required to develop in the subject you are reviewing. Then, write comments on your progress in each particular skill and on your knowledge and understanding of the various aspects or different topics of the subject.

- Think about your *coursework*. Identify what you consider to be your strengths and weaknesses, and comment on any particular difficulties or problems that have occurred.

- Think about the form of the *examination* and how you have been performing in practice tests and practice papers. Comment on your achievement in any oral or practical tests and in practice papers, focusing on the different types of questions that are set in the various papers e.g. multiple-choice questions, data-response questions, short-answer questions, essay-type questions.

ON YOUR OWN

Choose a subject about which you are concerned for some reason. Use the self-assessment guidelines either to write a report on your progress or to draw up a list of points for discussion with your teacher. Then, ask your subject teacher for an appointment. Compare your views of your progress with your teacher's views and agree a plan of action, setting targets for your improvement in that subject.

A subject I'm very concerned about is Maths. I work hard in lessons and do quite well in my homework, but I don't do so well in tests, because I tend to work too slowly and I run out of time. Also, I sometimes take rather a long time to grasp some mathematical equations and concepts. But I'm managing to make progress on the skills that are holding me back, by going over work when I have time, asking for extra work and generally trying to improve. — Peter.

Assessing your study skills

It is important also to review your study skills. If you know what your strengths and weaknesses are, it can help you to draw up plans to make your studying more effective. Below is a list of study skills that you need to develop.

ORGANISATIONAL SKILLS
Managing your time.
Looking after books and equipment.
Keeping your files in order.
Planning your revision.

READING SKILLS
Using the SQ3R strategy.
Identifying and interpreting bias.
Taking notes.
Making summaries.

WRITING SKILLS
Writing factual reports and essays.
Writing analytical essays.
Writing timed answers.
Spelling and punctuation.

ORAL SKILLS
Speaking and listening in groups.
Giving talks and presentations.
Preparing a speech for a debate.

RESEARCH SKILLS
Planning investigations and enquiries.
Locating information from different sources.
Collecting and recording data.
Interpreting and analysing data.
Evaluating data.

IT SKILLS
Using IT to locate and retrieve information.
Using IT to handle and process information.
Using IT tools to solve problems.
Using word processors and desk top publishing facilities.

ON YOUR OWN

Think about each of the study skills listed on this page. Use a 5-point scale to assess your strengths and weaknesses – 1 Very good 2 Good 3 Average 4 Weak 5 Very weak. Then, write a short statement summarising what your self-assessment tells you about your study skills.

Either make an appointment to see your tutor to discuss your statement or show your statement to a parent or friend. Talk about your strengths, then discuss together how you might set about trying to improve those of your study skills which are weak. Draw up an action plan, setting yourself targets and setting dates when you will review your progress in achieving those targets.

> As far as my study skills are concerned, I'm good at looking after my books and keeping my files in order but I'm bad at planning my time and organising my revision. These are things I need to work at improving.
> Also, I need to learn to write more concisely, because I tend to run out of time when I do tests and my teachers say that this is because my answers tend to be too long-winded and I don't stick closely enough to the point.
> One of my strengths is my oral work. I enjoy joining in discussions and I don't mind standing up and telling people my views. I'm never worried about asking a question. — Rashid

RECORDING YOUR ACHIEVEMENTS

Towards the end of your course you will be asked to prepare a personal statement for your National Record of Achievement folder. The personal statement gives you an opportunity to record details of all your achievements both inside and outside school.

There are four stages you will need to follow in preparing your statement. The first is to carry out a review of your achievements. The second is to use a word processor to produce a draft of your statement. The third is to arrange an appointment with your tutor to discuss the statement. The fourth is to redraft the statement in the light of your teacher's comments and to print out the final version.

Stage 1 – Reviewing your achievements

This involves making notes of everything you have achieved during your secondary school career, both in and out of school. At this stage it is important to include anything at all which might be classified as an achievement, even if you are not sure whether it merits inclusion.

Use the questions (below) as prompts to help you to think of what you have achieved, and make lists of your achievements under the four different headings.

1 Academic achievements

Think about all the courses you are studying – both your exam courses and any non-examination courses.

Which are your strongest subjects?
What particular strengths and skills do you have in these subjects?
What skills have you shown in your course-work assignments?
How well did you do in the trial exams?
What grades do you realistically expect to achieve in the exams?
What subjects do you hope to continue to study next year?
What qualifications do you hope ultimately to achieve?

2 Work and work experience

Think about any experiences which you have had of working and the world of work.

What part-time job or jobs have you done?
What skills have you developed and what qualities have you shown in any part-time jobs you have done?

Where did you do your work experience?
What did you achieve or learn during your work experience?
Have you done any voluntary work?
What careers are you currently interested in?

3 School activities

Have you represented the school in any teams? e.g. sports teams. Have you been awarded any certificates for sporting achievements? e.g. gymnastics, athletics, swimming.
Have you taken part in any musical or dramatic performances or helped backstage with any productions?
Have you passed any music or speech and drama exams?
Have you been awarded any certificates for activities such as the Duke of Edinburgh's Award scheme?
Have you helped to organise any fund-raising activities for charity?
Have you been on any residential courses e.g. to an outdoor activities centre, or taken part in a foreign trip e.g. skiing or a foreign exchange trip?
Have you done any community service of any kind?
Have you been elected to any posts of responsibility e.g. form captain, school council representative?
Which school clubs and societies have you belonged to? Have you developed any skills through being a member?
Are there any other things that you have achieved at school? e.g. commendations for your service to the school or merit awards for the excellence of a particular project.

4 Out-of-school interests

What are your main out-of-school interests and activities?
What skills have you developed in your out-of-school activities?
Which clubs and organisations do you belong to?
What events have you taken part in?
Have you achieved anything special in your out-of-school activities? e.g. been chosen to represent your club or been awarded certificates.

Stage 2 – Drafting your report

Use a word processor to produce a draft of your statement based on the notes you have made. Start with details of the courses you are studying and of your academic achievements, then go on to explain what else you have achieved in and out of school.

Stage 3 – A discussion with your tutor

Show your draft statement to your tutor. Discuss each section of the statement to make sure there isn't anything important which you have left out, and ask for advice on things which you are not sure whether to include. Listen to what your tutor has to say and be prepared to alter what you have written if your tutor suggests you are underestimating or overestimating what you have achieved or what you expect to achieve in the exams.

Stage 4 – Writing and printing the statement

Redraft your statement, print out a copy and sign it. Then, give it to your tutor or head of year for them to sign to confirm that it is an accurate record of your achievements up to the age of 16.

My name is Mark Benson, and I am in year eleven, my last year, at High Heath School.

In year 10 I was chosen to go to Tagar Manor with the PE department, where I did a variety of activities, from rock climbing to canoeing and caving. It was extremely fun, and it taught me a lot about how to work in a team to overcome problems etc. I am going to Germany for a week with the school after my GCSEís, and I am looking forward to it greatly. I am also in the school badminton club. Out of school I have one big pastime, playing guitar (both acoustic and electric), which I fund through my two paper rounds. I have been having lessons for about six months, and been playing for a year now and I am getting quite good. I also enjoy listening to various types of music, from pop to American grunge.

When I started on the GCSE course I found that the amount of subjects I was doing decreased, but the time I spent on each increased, and also the attitude to the work we were doing got more serious. The subjects I have taken for my GCSEís are French, Maths, English Language and Literature, Design and Communication, Double Science, and Art and Design. In a lot of my subjects I get coursework, which is very important as my GCSE grades partly depend on it. I have been working hard on my coursework and am quite pleased with the results.

At the end of year 10, I had two weeks work experience with Emily Jones Graphical Services. It was very enjoyable and I learnt a lot about graphic design and the associated areas of work. Now in year 11, there is an increasing amount of careers work in PSE, and it is very relevant to me, but I have decided that I will stay on to the sixth form and do some A levels. I think my grades will be good enough, as my last reports (end of year 10) were Aís and Bís with one C. I have little idea what I will do after I leave the sixth form, but I will probably go to a college or university.

11 Thinking about careers

When you are considering what you might do for a career you need to think about three things: your strengths, your interests and your personal qualities.

The self-assessments you carry out in order to review your progress in your courses (see pages 48-49) will help you to identify some of your strengths. However, many people also have strengths and skills which they develop as a result of their interest in a particular hobby or activity. So when you are thinking about your interests, be aware of any particular expertise you may have developed which you might use in a career. Also, it is important to analyse your personal qualities and to see whether they match up with the personal qualities required for the careers which you are considering.

Reviewing your personal qualities

Look at the list below, and decide how many of these qualities – or their opposites – belong to you. Be honest and try to be self-critical. Most people have a mixture of good and not-so-good qualities. The more you recognise your own strengths and weaknesses, the more likely you are to be able to choose a suitable career.

> adventurous assertive calm
> careful competent concerned
> conscientious cooperative curious
> dependable easy-going enthusiastic
> flexible generous good-tempered
> hard-working honest humorous
> imaginative loyal open-minded
> patient persevering polite punctual
> questioning reliable resourceful
> self-confident sincere sympathetic
> tidy tolerant

ON YOUR OWN

Use the list of words to help you to review your personal qualities. Then, write a statement about yourself similar to the statements which Coretta and Tim wrote about themselves. When you have finished, show your statement to someone who knows you well – a parent, a teacher or a friend – and see if they agree that it is a true reflection of your personal qualities.

The best thing about me is that I'm very friendly – I can get on with anyone if I want to. I can hold back my temper, too. One thing that might offend people is that I'm really upfront. I come right out and say what I mean. I'd like to work looking after children – child-minding or in a nursery. I can understand children. I know how to talk to them and I'm very caring. I'll do a two-year course and at the end I'll get a certificate. It means I'm a responsible person and qualified to look after children. Coretta (16)

My personality's O.K. I mix with lots of different people and I make mates easily. I think I'm alright really. I get on well with people of my age, but not older people like my parents. My bad side is that I'm normally lazy and I can't be bothered to do things. I hope to get at least five good GCSEs. I'd like to go to Art college to do a course in graphic design. Then I'd like to work in advertising. It's well paid. I reckon I'll have to stop being lazy and work harder, though. – Tim (14)

Below are details of the sort of qualities and abilities you need in certain areas of work. There are also a number of qualities that are required in all areas of work, such as reliability, honesty, perseverance, the ability to keep your temper and a good sense of humour.

IN PAIRS

Study the qualities and abilities required for each area of work. Think about your own qualities and abilities. In which area of work do your qualities and abilities seem to match most closely those that are required?

What other areas of work can you think of? Each choose an area that you are interested in. List the qualities and abilities that you need for that area of work. Discuss how closely your qualities and abilities match those that are needed.

Office work

You need to be:
- ✔ a good and efficient organiser.
- ✔ neat and methodical.
- ✔ good at spelling and punctuation.
- ✔ good with figures.
- ✔ able to get on with people.
- ✔ happy with a routine.

Creative work

You need to be:
- ✔ imaginative and articulate.
- ✔ artistic.
- ✔ flexible.
- ✔ happy working under pressure.

Technical and Scientific work

You need to be:
- ✔ interested in problem solving.
- ✔ able to work in a team.
- ✔ practical and methodical.
- ✔ good with numbers and calculations.

Caring work

You need to be:
- ✔ interested in people and their problems.
- ✔ prepared to work for lowish wages.
- ✔ sympathetic but firm-minded.
- ✔ able to remain calm in emergency situations.

Construction work

You need to be:
- ✔ happy working outdoors.
- ✔ physically fit.
- ✔ good with your hands.
- ✔ able to take orders.
- ✔ able to work as part of a team.

Service work (shops, catering etc.)

You need to be:
- ✔ able to get on with people.
- ✔ willing to be on your feet most of the time.
- ✔ prepared to wear some sort of uniform.
- ✔ good with figures.
- ✔ honest and reliable.

FINDING OUT ABOUT DIFFERENT JOBS

When you are researching different jobs, it is useful to have a list of questions that you want to answer. This will help you to record all the information you find out. Below is a Job Factsheet listing questions that you might want answered by your research.

ON YOUR OWN

Choose one or two careers in which you are currently interested. Use the careers library and other sources of information to answer the questions in the Job Factsheet. Then put the completed factsheets together to create a Jobs Factfile to which all the members of your group can refer.

J O B   F A C T S H E E T

Name of job

Researched by   Date

1   What particular activities does this job require you to do? (For example, a journalist is involved in researching, interviewing, writing, editing and proofreading.)

2   What sort of place would you be working in? (For example, would you be working indoors or outdoors? in an office, out on site, in a factory, a shop or somewhere else?)

3   Would you be working on your own or with others?

4   List the particular qualities and skills you require for this career.

5   What qualifications do you need in order to apply for this particular job?

6   Where can you get the necessary training, education or experience for this job?

7   Are there any particular restrictions about this career? (For example, do you have to be over a certain age? Do you need a driving licence? Are there any medical restrictions, such as not being colour blind?)

8   What are the rewards of this job? (For example, high salary, flexible working hours, challenges, excitement, fulfilment.)

9   What is the career structure in this type of work? Are there plenty of opportunities for promotion?

10   What is the competition like for this type of job? Are there plenty of jobs available or are there a lot of people competing for a few jobs?

11   Where are there opportunities for this type of job? (e.g. Only in large cities or where certain companies are located?)

12   What steps do you need to take now, if you are interested in this career? (For example, are there any subjects you need to go on studying or any courses you need to apply for?)

13   Now that you have researched it, give the reasons why you think you would or would not find this type of career satisfying.

Learning from advertisements

••••DRAUGHTSPERSON••••

We require a draughtsperson to work in our busy Drawing Office which produces engineering drawing packages. The work is varied and involves the production of manufacturing drawings, checking drawings, handling associated production control information and processing modification requests. This position requires someone with good liaison skills who can interact successfully with people at all levels within the Company and work effectively in a team. Candidates should have a sound practical engineering background, and an aptitude for mechanical design. Good organisation and communication skills are essential. Candidates must be able to demonstrate good engineering drawing skills, and have some experience of using CAD systems. Recognised qualifications in mechanical engineering are desirable.

IN PAIRS

Study the job advertisements on this page. For each one, make a list of the particular qualities, skills and aptitudes you need for that job. Then, discuss your own strengths and skills and say whether you think you would or would not be capable of doing that job.

Each find an advertisement for a career in which you are interested. What qualities, skills and aptitudes does the advertisement require in applicants? What qualifications do applicants need to have? Compare the requirements with your own strengths and skills and discuss how you could obtain any qualifications that are required.

Receptionist

£10,000 per annum

Key Duties/Responsibilities
- ☞ Receive clients
- ☞ Answer telephone
- ☞ Maintain client records and files
- ☞ Ensure reception area is presentable

Essential Qualities
- ☞ Pleasant and helpful manner
- ☞ Able to deal with a variety of people
- ☞ Organised and tidy
- ☞ Literate and numerate

Recreation Assistant
£11,500

Energetic, enthusiastic, team worker required for supervising the recreational and poolside areas of new leisure centre. The job will involve the responsibility of setting up of all equipment around the pool and ensuring that all areas are kept safe and tidy. A life saving qualification is essential and the RLSS National Pool lifeguard qualification would be desirable. A certificate in first aid would be advantageous, but suitable candidates without this will be considered with a view to training. Good communication skills are essential.
You will be working an average of 40 hours per week which will include evenings and weekends.

APPRENTICESHIP
Service and Maintenance Engineer

Two suitable applicants with at least four GCSEs, including Maths and Technology, are required to undertake a specialist four-year apprenticeship course.
The successful applicants will be trained and educated at college to be fully qualified Service & Maintenance Engineers. The job scope will cover air conditioning, refrigeration and electrical services.
Applicants should have a practical aptitude, interest in working with their hands and an enquiring mind.

Assistant Care Worker

An assistant is required to support the care workers at Greenoaks old people's home. The work would involve dressing, washing and feeding of old people. Some cleaning work will also be involved.
Previous experience or a GNVQ in Health and Social Care is desirable. A caring attitude, and a pleasant and bright manner is essential.

INVESTIGATING CAREERS

There are several other ways of investigating careers besides studying the information that is available in libraries and resource centres. Three other ways of learning about what a job involves are: talking to people, visiting workplaces and doing voluntary work.

1 Talk to someone who is doing the job.

You may already know someone who works in the career area that you are interested in. If so, do not be afraid to approach them to ask them about their job and the qualifications that are needed to do it. Many people are fascinated by their work and will be only too willing to talk to you about it. To make full use of the opportunity of talking to someone, prepare for the conversation as you would prepare for an interview, by making a list of the information you want to discover and the questions you want to ask. If you do not know someone, then use your initiative. You can always telephone a local firm and see if there is someone, such as a personnel officer, who would be willing to spare some of their time to talk to you.

2 Arrange to visit a workplace.

One of your parents, relatives or friends may be able to arrange for you to visit their workplace, so that you can see for yourself what a particular job involves. Alternatively, you may be able to go on a conducted tour. Large firms and places such as power stations and newspaper offices often offer guided tours at set times to visitors. Either contact the firm directly or ask at your local tourist office for details of workplaces that you can visit. Again, use your initiative. If you are really interested in visiting somewhere, it's worth the cost of a phone call to ring up and ask if it is possible to arrange a visit.

When you go on a visit or tour, make full use of it by asking questions, writing down anything important you need to remember, and collecting any pamphlets or brochures that can give you further information.

3 Offer to do some voluntary work.

Nothing can provide you with more insight into what a job involves than first-hand experience. In certain types of job it may be possible for you to spend some time doing voluntary work. For example, if you are interested in care work with elderly people, it might be possible for you to arrange to work as a volunteer at a day centre for elderly people or in a residential home. As a volunteer you can observe the kind of work that the care staff have to do and you will be able to find out whether or not you would like a job in that area. Once again, it's up to you to take the initiative and to enquire if there is any way you can volunteer so as to get experience of what a job involves.

Tracy's story

Tracy thought she might like to be a lawyer. She'd seen lots of trials on TV, but wondered what a court room was really like, so she spent a morning watching the proceedings at the local magistrate's court. She found it very interesting, so she decided to find out more. She asked about and found that one of her classmates had an aunt who worked in a solicitor's office, so she contacted the aunt and went round one evening for a chat. Before she went, she drew up a list of questions to ask about the work that is done in a solicitor's office. She was surprised to learn that different firms specialised in different types of law. Her friend's aunt said that it might be possible for Tracy to spend a day at the solicitor's office shadowing her at work. Two weeks later Tracy spent a day in the solicitor's office. Everything she learned about how a law firm works and what a lawyer does convinced her that she'd like either to become a lawyer or to work in a solicitor's office. It made her determined to work hard to pass her exams and helped her to make up her mind which A levels to choose.

ON YOUR OWN

Use your initiative and arrange either to talk to someone who works in a career in which you are currently interested, to visit a workplace, to spend a day shadowing someone at work or to do some voluntary work. When you have done so, write a short statement to put in your file saying what you learned from the experience.

LEARNING FROM YOUR WORK EXPERIENCE

Many schools offer 15 and 16-year-olds the opportunity of doing one or two weeks' work experience. Wherever you get a placement, you cannot expect to do precisely the type of work that you would eventually hope to be doing in that job. After all, you haven't got the qualifications or the experience, so you can only expect to do the work that someone in a junior position might be asked to do. However, you can learn a lot from observing and talking to people about their work.

It is a good idea to keep a work experience diary and to spend some time each evening recording your experiences. You can then use the diary as the basis for a longer piece of writing when you are back in school, analysing and evaluating what you learned from your work experience.

ON YOUR OWN

Study Teresa's account of her work experience and then write a similar account saying what you learned from your work experience.

IN GROUPS

Show each other your accounts of your work experience and discuss what you learned from it.

1

My work placement was in a bank. I was pleased when I found out where I was going, because I'd been thinking about working in a bank or a building society as a possible career.

I spent the evening before my first day ironing my shirt, because I wanted to look smart. I was looking forward to doing something new and different, but I was a bit apprehensive about being around so many adults, because I'm quite a shy person.

The first day I didn't start until ten o'clock. I wasn't sure where to go, so I went up to the counter and asked one of the staff, who invited me into the office to wait. My first impressions were how busy everyone seemed to be.

I was shown round the building, which has four floors, and told the fire procedure. Then I spent the first day working in an office with someone called Karen. The jobs I had to do were sorting out cheques, looking for lost cheques and using the adding up machine to balance credits and debits. I left at five o'clock and was pleased to get home as the day had seemed quite long.

The next day I had to be there at nine o'clock. I was hoping to do something more interesting than the day before, but I ended up doing the same things, as well as odd jobs like photocopying.

On the Wednesday I was told to work on the ground floor by the cashiers' desks. I spent the morning working with a man called Justin, but I didn't enjoy it, because he kept using a lot of bank jargon and I found it difficult to follow his instructions. In the afternoon, I worked with a lady called Alison on the computers, opening accounts for people, and I found that more interesting.

2

On the Thursday, I was given something completely different to do. I had to visit all the other banks and building societies in the town and ask questions about their opening hours and Saturday services. I then wrote up all the information on a computer and printed out copies. I quite enjoyed doing this, as I felt I was doing something important, and my supervisor, Thomas, seemed really pleased with the end result.

Friday and the second week were mainly spent doing odd jobs like filing, addressing envelopes, photocopying, sorting cheques and vouchers, printing statements, and balancing books. I also got to use the computer quite a lot and once did some typing from dictation, which I wasn't very good at.

One of my most valuable experiences was probably attending meetings, which gave me a proper insight into life in banking and the sort of problems that the staff had to deal with.

By the end of the two weeks I'd got to know everyone who worked there and they were very friendly and patient with me. But I was quite relieved when the fortnight ended, because some of the work was quite tedious and I felt rather tired at the end of each day.

I learned a lot from the experience about what it's like to work in an office and what skills you need. I'm not sure that I want to work in bank, though, because I didn't find the work as interesting as I thought I would.

Teresa Plant

12 Choosing your courses

At 16+ there are a number of options open to you:

- You can continue in full-time education either at school or at a college. If you decide to study full-time, you are entitled to a free place and will not have to pay any fees.

- You can apply to continue your education part-time at a college. However, you may find that you have to pay fees.

- You can leave school to go straight into employment. If you decide to do so, you may be able to get a youth training place in which you get training for a particular type of job. On the other hand, you may not be able to find a job or one that offers you any training.

CHOOSING YOUR PATHWAY

The majority of young people between the ages of 16 and 19 decide to continue in full-time or part-time education and training. There are a wide range of courses available, but basically there are three main pathways you can follow in order to try to obtain qualifications.

1 General education

You continue studying at school or at a college. You can do a one-year course in order to get more GCSEs or to improve your GCSE grades. Or you can do a two-year course leading to A level and AS level qualifications.

2 Vocational education

You follow a vocational educational course at school or college. You can do a GNVQ (General National Vocational Qualification) or GSVQ (General Scottish Vocational Qualification) course at either Foundation, Intermediate or Advanced level. The course may be full-time or part-time and be for either one or two years.

3 Vocational training

You receive training for a particular type of job. If you get a youth training place you will do either an NVQ (National Vocational Qualification) or an SVQ (Scottish Vocational Qualification) course. This may be a full-time or part-time, for one or two years, and the training may be either at work or in college.

Although there are three pathways, you can often combine different kinds of qualifications in a single course of study. For example, if you are a full-time student, you may be able to take one or two GCSEs, while studying for a Foundation or Intermediate level GNVQ.

Similarly, it is possible to move from one pathway to another. After doing an Intermediate level GNVQ, you may be able to take GCSE A levels. It is increasingly likely that, in future, many people will take NVQs and SVQs at work, whatever other qualifications they obtain before starting employment.

The chart (below) shows the qualifications framework and how you can move from one pathway to another. The other pages in this unit give further information on each pathway to help you to decide which pathway you should choose at 16+.

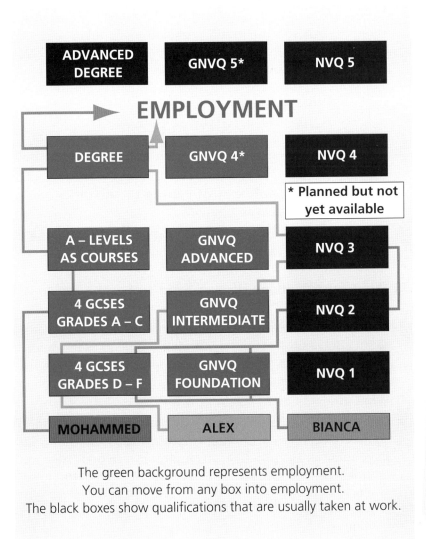

The green background represents employment.
You can move from any box into employment.
The black boxes show qualifications that are usually taken at work.

IN PAIRS

Study the chart. Talk about the different pathways which Mohammed, Alex and Bianca followed at 16+, and how Alex moved between the pathways.

Dear Gita
I can't make up my mind whether to stay on at school or leave and go to college. I'm worried that if I go to college I'll find it hard to settle in, though the course there looks attractive. What are the most important things to consider before I make up my mind? I'm confused.

Geoffrey (16)

Where to Study – School or College?

If you want to continue your full-time education, you may have to decide whether to stay on at school or leave and go to college. In some cases, the decision may be made for you because the course you want to follow is only available at one of them.

If you do have a choice, don't be influenced too much by what your friends are going to do. Weigh up the pros and cons, talk to people who have stayed on at school and people who have left to go to college. Find out all you can about college life and compare it to school life. Then, make your own decision, based on what's right for you.

IN PAIRS

Make lists of the advantages and disadvantages of a) staying on at school b) going to college. Then, draft a reply to Geoffrey's letter.

A LEVELS

Q How many people choose A level courses?

A About one in three people aged 16-18 are doing A level courses.

Q Why do so many people choose A level courses?

A Many people choose A level courses in order to obtain the qualifications they need for Higher Education courses e.g. degree courses at Universities. The minimum requirement for degree courses is usually two good A level grades. But there is fierce competition for places on many degree courses, especially in certain popular subjects, such as English, and in some specialist subjects, such as medicine. For some degree courses, therefore, the entry requirement is good grades in three A level subjects.

A levels are also a recognised way of obtaining the qualifications required for courses leading to professional qualifications in many areas ranging from accountancy to physiotherapy.

Q Are A levels the only way of getting the qualifications you need for a degree course?

A No, you can obtain a place on a degree course by doing Advanced GNVQs or a course that combines A level qualifications and GNVQ qualifications.

Q What qualifications do you need to be able to do A levels?

A You are usually expected to have got at least a GCSE grade C in that subject or a related subject. The main requirement for you to start a 3 A level course is usually good GCSE grades – C or above – in at least four subjects.

Q What subjects can you do at A level?

A There are A level courses in almost 400 subjects including such subjects as Accountancy, Law, Theatre Studies and Psychology. In practice, though, you won't have a completely free choice. You will be restricted to those subjects that are offered by the schools and colleges in your area.

Many students choose two or three A level subjects in related areas of the curriculum e.g. Physics, Chemistry and Biology. But you do not have to do so. Combinations of unrelated subjects, such as French, Maths and History are acceptable as entry qualifications for many Higher Education courses.

Q What are AS levels?

A An AS level course covers only half an A level syllabus. So qualifications in two AS level courses are usually regarded as the equivalent of an A level qualification in one subject. It is often possible, therefore, for you to take a course consisting of 2 A levels and 2 AS levels. The advantage of

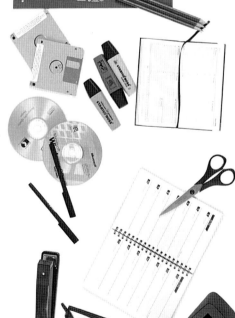

taking AS levels is that you can do a broader range of courses and keep up a subject that you would otherwise have had to drop. Again, your choice will be limited by what is on offer in the schools and colleges in your area.

Q Are A and AS level courses very different from GCSE courses?

A They are more demanding and far more intensive. The type of work you do will vary from subject to subject, but you will have to read widely and you will study aspects of the subject in much greater depth and in more detail than you did for GCSE. In many subjects, you will have to write detailed analytical essays.

Q How are A levels assessed and examined? Is there any coursework?

A The amount of coursework varies. Some A levels are modular courses and you are assessed at the end of each module. However, most A level assessment is by the end-of-course written examination, with oral and practical exams in some subjects.

Q If I get the necessary minimum qualifications, should I definitely do A levels?

A If you only get the minimum qualifications, then you need to consider very carefully whether a 3 A level course is the right course for you. A level courses are very academic and a 3 A level course may not be suitable for you. A GNVQ course or a course combining one A level with an intermediate or advanced GNVQ may be a better option.

> I'm glad I chose a 3 A level course. It's hard work, but I've always enjoyed reading and I find the essay-writing and discussions in seminars really stimulating.
> —Jeneva.

> I did well enough at GCSE to be accepted on the A level course. But I'm beginning to wonder if I made the right choice. The work is very academic and I'm finding it hard to cope.
> —Alain

High Rewards, High Risk

There's a lot to be said in favour of A levels if you've got the ability and you enjoy academic study and are good at examinations. A levels have high status and they provide a passport to Higher Education and a wide range of professional careers. But there are a number of drawbacks. Because you are only studying 3 subjects, you are getting rather a narrow education. Also, although it is possible to choose vocational subjects at A level (e.g. Accounting, Law), many A level subjects do not give you the practical skills and the training for jobs in the way that a GNVQ course would. There is, therefore, a considerable degree of risk involved if you decide to follow the A level path. If you pass and get good grades, the rewards can be high. But if you fail, you may find that you have got very little to show for two years' work.

IN PAIRS

Study the information on these two pages, then list what you consider to be the advantages and the drawbacks of A level courses.

Discuss whether or not you are thinking of applying for an A level course and give your reasons.

ON YOUR OWN

Find out by looking at the prospectuses for your school and your local college, which A level subjects are offered in your area. Study the details of the A level courses in those subjects in which you are interested.

GNVQs

GNVQs and GSVQs are vocational education courses. The courses are designed to help you to understand the world of work, to develop skills you will need in a particular area of work and to give you qualifications that will help you to go on either to further education and training or into employment. You choose a course that will train you to work in a particular vocational area, but not for a specific job.

GNVQS - A GUIDE FOR STUDENTS

About GNVQs

GNVQs are about work but are studied at school or college and not in the workplace.

GNVQs are about skills such as communicating and using numbers and technology.

GNVQs allow you and your tutors to devise a programme of learning to suit you.

GNVQs are unique in giving you:

- a broad understanding of a particular area of work such as engineering or health;
- skills which are essential to every career;
- the flexibility to take an A or AS level, additional units (for instance a modern foreign language), or an NVQ (National Vocational Qualification) alongside your GNVQ;
- credit for each unit of the GNVQ as it is taken, so that you have the option of changing subject or returning to your GNVQ after a break.

The range of subjects

GNVQs are available in the following vocational areas:

- Art and Design
- Science
- Business
- Engineering
- Health and Social Care
- Hospitality and Catering
- Leisure and Tourism
- Information Technology
- Manufacturing
- Management Studies
- Built Environment
- Media and Communications
- Land-based and Environmental Industries
- Retail and Distribution
- Performing Arts

The Levels

GNVQs are available at three levels:

1 **Foundation GNVQs** provide a broad introduction to a vocational area and normally take one year of full-time study.
2 **Intermediate GNVQs** are broadly equivalent to four or five GCSEs at grades A-C and normally take one year of full-time study.
3 **Advanced GNVQs** are broadly equivalent to two A levels and normally take two years of full-time study.

Entry qualifications

Entry to GNVQ courses is flexible, but as a guide:

- you do not usually need any qualifications to take a Foundation GNVQ course;
- you usually need one or two GCSEs at grades A to D, or a Foundation GNVQ, to take an Intermediate GNVQ course;
- you usually need four or five GCSEs at grades A to C, or an Intermediate GNVQ to take an Advanced GNVQ course.

Course structure

GNVQs are made up of units. Some of these concern the skills and knowledge essential to a particular area of work and others concern the core skills – communication, working with numbers and information technology – which are essential to every career.

GNVQs involve activities, projects and written tests. As part of a GNVQ, you might plan an event or carry out a market survey, or you might write a business proposal for a real or imaginary product. Each student has to produce a portfolio. The portfolio needs to contain a variety of evidence of your achievements, e.g. a written report, a videotape of a presentation or the testimony of a manager at your work placement.

You will have an action plan to help you meet the standards and to collect the right material to show that you have covered a particular unit.

Assessment

Your portfolio of evidence is assessed as you go along. There are also one-hour tests for those units which are a compulsory part of the course. The tests consist of short answers or multiple-choice questions. You must pass the tests in order to qualify for the full award, but they are set at frequent intervals and there are opportunities for you to retake a test, if you need to do so.

After GNVQs

After you have passed a GNVQ, you can either go on to the next GNVQ level, transfer to the academic pathway and go on to do GCSEs, A levels or a degree, or go into employment, with the option of taking an NVQ if one is available. (See the qualifications framework on page 59.)

•• IN PAIRS ••

Study the information on this page. Draw up a list of *Ten things you need to know if you're thinking of doing a GNVQ course.*

• ON YOUR OWN •

Do some more research about GNVQs. Interview some people who are doing GNVQ courses. Find books and leaflets about GNVQ in the resources centre e.g. *GNVQ Is it for you?* by Windsor Chorlton. Then write an article of between 250 and 400 words for a teenage magazine entitled *GNVQ – The real story.*

What GNVQ students say

❛It's the best choice I ever made. It's not at all like what we had to do for GCSE. It's much more practical. You're not cooped up in the classroom all the time. I feel I'm learning skills that will be really useful to me. ❜

❛What I like about GNVQs is that you get credit for each of the units you pass. And if you don't manage to pass a test first time, you can always take it again. ❜

❛I've been surprised at how hard it's been. When I said I was going to do an Advanced GNVQ rather than A levels, my friends thought I was taking the easy option. I can assure you, they were wrong! ❜

❛It's not what I expected. There's too much paperwork. I'm not sure I'll finish the course. ❜

NVQs

If you decide to leave school to go straight into employment, then it's well worth finding out what opportunities there are for you to do an NVQ. NVQs are available in a wide range of occupations and there are a number of advantages to doing an NVQ:

- It will train you in the specific skills you need in order to do a particular job.

- There are different levels and you can start at the level that is appropriate for you and work your way up. In practice, most 16-year-old school-leavers start at level 1 or level 2. But if you have the ability and apply yourself, you can end up with equivalent qualifications to those achieved by people who continue in full-time education.

- They are recognised and valued by most employers.

- The government is keen to encourage young people to train, so you can get government money for training, provided that you are going to reach NVQ level 2. The money is called a youth credit and is for you to spend on a college course, training at work or evening classes.

However, the drawback with NVQs is that most of them are only available to you if you have a job or have regular access to a workplace.

WHAT ARE THE DIFFERENCES BETWEEN NVQS AND GNVQS?

Comparative features of GNVQs and NVQs		
	GNVQs	NVQs
Aimed at	full-time students	mainly employees and some students
Develop	general vocational skills and understanding	occupational competence
Assessed	mainly outside workplace	in workplace or simulated workplace
Standards developed by	NCVQ and awarding bodies	employers
Courses available	limited number in each vocational area	wide number in each occupational area

HOW CAN I FIND OUT MORE ABOUT NVQs?

You can find out more about NVQs from your local Training and Enterprise Council or your local careers office. Alternatively, you can write to one of the three main awarding bodies – BTEC, City and Guilds or RSA – or the National Council for Vocational Qualifications (NCVQ).

Dear Gita,
I'm leaving school as soon as my exams are over to try and get a job. My teachers say I should try and get one that gives me the chance to do an NVQ. I'm fed up with education, but I want to get on in a career. Should I do an NVQ or not?

Laurie

IN PAIRS

Discuss what you have learned about NVQs from the information on this page. What are the advantages of doing an NVQ for someone who wants to leave school at 16? Draft a reply to Laurie's letter.

ON YOUR OWN

Either contact your local Training and Enterprise Council to find out about NVQ opportunities in your area or write to the NCVQ to find out more about NVQs.

USEFUL ADDRESSES

BTEC
Central House
Upper Woburn Place
London WC1H 0HH

RSA Examinations Board
Westwood Way
Coventry CV4 8HS

City and Guilds of London Institute
46 Britannia Street
London WC1X 9RG

National Council for Vocational Qualifications
222 Euston Road
London NW1 2BZ